THE COLLECTED WORKS
OF AMBROSE BIERCE

VOLUME IV

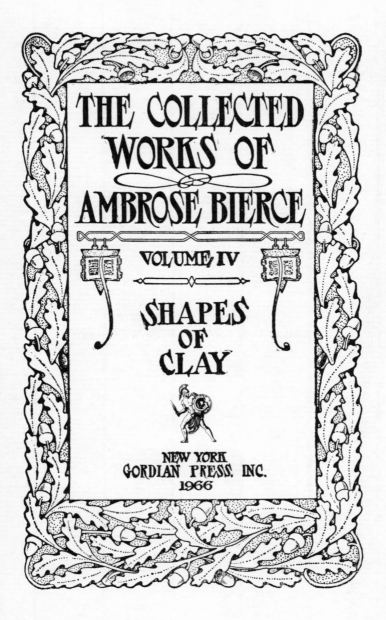

THE COLLECTED WORKS OF AMBROSE BIERCE

VOLUME IV

SHAPES OF CLAY

NEW YORK
GORDIAN PRESS, INC.
1966

Originally Published 1910
Reprinted 1966

Published by
GORDIAN PRESS, INC.

Library of Congress Card Catalog No. 66-14638

Printed in the U.S.A. by
EDWARDS BROTHERS, INC.
Ann Arbor, Michigan

PREFACE

OF the verses republished in this volume and the next, some are censorious, and in these the names of real persons are used without their consent; so it seems fit that a few words be said of the matter in sober prose. Of my motive in writing and now republishing these personal satires I do not care to make either defense or explanation, except with reference to those, who, since my first censure of them, have passed away. To one having only a reader's interest in the matter it may seem that the verses relating to those might properly have been omitted from this collection. But if these pieces, or, indeed, any considerable part of my work in literature, have the intrinsic interest, which, by this attempt to preserve some of it I have assumed, their permanent suppression is impossible; it is only a question of when and by whom they will be republished. Some one will surely search them out and put them into circulation.

I conceive it to be the right of an author to have his fugitive work in newspapers and periodicals put into a more permanent form during his lifetime if he can; and this is especially true of one whose work, necessarily engendering animosities, is peculiarly exposed to challenge as unjust. That is a charge that can best be examined before time has effaced the evidence. For the death of a man whose unworth I have affirmed, I am in no way accountable, and however sincerely I may regret his pass-

6 1

ing, I can hardly be expected to consent that it shall affect my literary fortunes. If the satirist who does not accept the remarkable doctrine that while condemning a sin he should spare the sinner were bound to let the life of his work be coterminous with that of his subject his lot in letters were one of peculiar hardship.

Persuaded of the validity of all this, I have not hesitated to reprint even certain " epitaphs," which, once of the living, are now of the dead, as all the others must eventually be. The objection inheres in all forms of applied satire—my understanding of whose laws, liberties and limitations, is at least derived from reverent study of the masters. That in respect of matters herein mentioned I have followed their practice can be shown by abundant instance and example.

In arranging these verses for publication I have thought it needless to classify them as " serious," " comic," " sentimental," " satirical," and so forth. I do the reader the honor to think that he will readily discern the character of what he is reading, and I entertain the hope that his mood will accommodate itself without disappointment to that of his author.

AMBROSE   BIERCE.

CONTENTS

PAGE

PREFACE 9

SHAPES OF CLAY.

THE PASSING SHOW.... 19
ELIXIR VITÆ 22
CONVALESCENT 24
AT THE CLOSE OF THE
CANVASS 26
GEOTHEOS 28
POLITICS 29
THE VALLEY OF DRY
BONES 30
POLYPHEMUS 31
IN DEFENSE 32
INVOCATION 34
RELIGION 39
TWO SOCIALISTS 40
A MORNING FANCY...... 42
VISIONS OF SIN......... 44
GENIUS 46
THE TOWN OF DÆ..... 47
AN ANARCHIST 53
AN OFFER OF MAR-
RIAGE 54
ARMA VIRUMQUE 57
ON A PROPOSED CREMA-
TORY 57

PAGE

A DEMAND 59
THE WEATHER-WIGHT.. 61
T. A. H.............. 67
MY MONUMENT 68
MAD 68
FOR COERCION OF CO-
LOMBIA 70
A TEAGOING ADMIRAL... 72
THE WOOER 74
SILHOUETTES OF ORIEN-
TALS 76
LAND OF THE PILGRIM'S
PRIDE 78
A SINGLE TERMER...... 80
A PLAGUE OF ASSES..... 81
IN CUBA 82
FOR A CERTAIN CRITIC.. 85
ARTHUR MCEWEN....... 87
CHARLES AND PETER.... 87
CONTEMPLATION 89
THE GOLDEN AGE...... 90
A PROPHET OF PEACE.... 92
AN UNREFORMABLE RE-
FORMER 93
THE WORD-WAY IN PAN-
AMA 95

CONTENTS

PAGE

THE JACK OF CLUBS.... 98
A NAVAL METHOD...... 99
ANOTHER ASPIRANT 102
A LEARNER 103
TO BRIDGET 104
AFTER TENNYSON 105
TO MY BIRD...........106
BUSINESS 108
A POSSIBILITY 109
TO A CENSOR...........110
"THE WHOLE WORLD
    KIN" 113
A FUTURE CONVERSATION.113
THE HESITATING VET-
    ERAN 115
A YEAR'S "CASUALTIES".118
TO-DAY 118
AN ALIBI 120
A MEETING 127
J. F. B...............129
THE DYING STATESMAN.129
THE DEATH OF GRANT..131
THE FOUNTAIN REFILLED.132
LAUS LUCIS 138
NANINE 139
TECHNOLOGY 140
A REPLY TO A LETTER. 142
TO OSCAR WILDE.......144
BORN LEADERS OF MEN..145
THE CRIME OF 1903....146
FOR EXPULSION 148

PAGE

JUDEX JOCOSUS 150
"GRAFT" 151
THE TALE OF A CRIME.151
TO THE BARTHOLDI
    STATUE 153
AN UNMERRY CHRIST-
    MAS 155
FROM VIRGINIA TO PARIS..157
A "MUTE INGLORIOUS
    MILTON" 158
THE FREE TRADER'S LA-
    MENT 159
SUBTERRANEAN PHANTA-
    SIES 160
IN MEMORIAM 163
THE STATESMAN 165
BROTHERS 168
THE CYNIC'S BEQUEST...169
CORRECTED NEWS 177
MR. FINK'S DEBATING
    DONKEY 178
TO MY LAUNDRESS......183
FAME 184
OMNES VANITAS 186
CONSOLATION 186
FATE 187
PHILOSOPHER BIMM 187
REMINDED 189
SALVINI IN AMERICA....190
ANOTHER WAY 193
ART 193

CONTENTS

PAGE

TO ONE ACROSS THE
WAY 194
TO A DEBTOR ABROAD...195
GENESIS 195
LIBERTY 196
THE PASSING OF SHEP-
HERD 197
TO MAUDE 200
THE BIRTH OF VIRTUE..201
THE SCURRIL PRESS.....201
STANLEY 204
ONE OF THE UNFAIR SEX.205
THE LORD'S PRAYER ON
A COIN 206
AD ABSURDUM 206
SAITH THE CZAR........208
THE ROYAL JESTER.....209
A CAREER IN LETTERS...213
THE FOLLOWING PAIR...214
POLITICAL ECONOMY 215
THE UNPARDONABLE SIN..216
INDUSTRIAL DISCONTENT..218
TEMPORA MUTANTUR ...219
A FALSE ALARM 220
CONTENTMENT 221
CONSTANCY 223
THE NEW ENOCH ARDEN.224
DISAVOWAL 226
AN AVERAGE 227
INCURABLE 228
THE PUN 228

PAGE

TO NANINE 230
VICE VERSA 230
A BLACKLIST 232
AUTHORITY 232
THE PSORIAD 233
PEACE 237
THANKSGIVING 237
L'AUDACE 240
THE GOD'S VIEW-POINT..241
THE ÆSTHETES 245
WITH MINE OWN PE-
TARD 246
RESTORED 247
SIRES AND SONS........249
A CHALLENGE 249
TWO SHOWS 251
A POET'S HOPE........252
THE WOMAN AND THE
DEVIL 254
TWO ROGUES 255
THE PIED PIPER OF
BROOKLYN 257
NOT GUILTY 257
PRESENTIMENT 258
A STUDY IN GRAY......259
FOR MERIT 261
A BIT OF SCIENCE......261
THE TABLES TURNED...262
TO A DEJECTED POET...263
THE HUMORIST 264
MONTEFIORE 265

CONTENTS

	PAGE		PAGE
DISCRETION	266	LUSUS POLITICUS	299
AN EXILE	266	BEREAVEMENT	301
THE DIVISION SUPERIN-		A PICKBRAIN	302
TENDENT	267	THE NAVAL CONSTRUC-	
TO A PROFESSIONAL EU-		TOR	302
LOGIST	268	DETECTED	304
ELECTION DAY	270	BIMETALISM	304
THE MILITIAMAN	271	TWO METHODS	306
A WELCOME	272	FOUNDATIONS OF THE	
A SERENADE	273	STATE	306
THE WISE AND GOOD	274	AN IMPOSTOR	308
THE LOST COLONEL	275	FRANCE	309
FOR TAT	278	A GUEST	310
A DILEMMA	279	A FALSE PROPHECY	311
METEMPSYCHOSIS	281	A SONG OF THE MANY	312
THE SAINT AND THE		ONE MORNING	313
MONK	281	THE KING OF BORES	313
IN HIGH LIFE	283	HISTORY	314
A WHIPPER-IN	284	THE HERMIT	315
JUDGMENT	286	THE YEARLY LIE	317
A BUBBLE	286	AN APOLOGUE	318
FRANCINE	288	DIAGNOSIS	319
AN EXAMPLE	289	FALLEN	319
REVENGE	289	DIES IRÆ	320
THE GENESIS OF EMBAR-		ONE MOOD'S EXPRESSION	326
RASSMENT	291	SOMETHING IN THE PA-	
IN CONTUMACIAM	292	PERS	327
FROM THE MINUTES	292	THE BINNACLE	328
A WOMAN IN POLITICS	294	ONE PRESIDENT	329
A BALLAD OF PIKEVILLE	295	THE BRIDE	329
AN AUGURY	298	THE MAN BORN BLIND	330

CONTENTS

	PAGE
A Nightmare	333
A Wet Season	333
The Confederate Flags.	335
Hæc Fabula Docet	337
Again	338
Homo Podunkensis	340
A Social Call	341
My Day of Life	342

SOME ANTE-MORTEM EPITAPHS

A King of Craft	347
Stephen Dorsey	348
Mr. Justice Field	349
General B. F. Butler	349
Reparation	350
Disincorporated	350
A Kit	351
Disjunctus	351
A Trencher-Knight	351
A Vice-President	352
A Wasted Life	353

THE SCRAP HEAP

Poesy	357
Hospitality	357
Magnanimity	357
Understated	358
An Attorney-General	358
Financial News	358
Aspiration	359
Democracy	359

	PAGE
An Enemy to Law and Order	359
Foresight	360
A Fair Division	360
A Lacking Factor	360
The Politician	361
Elihu Root	361
An Error	361
Vanished at Cock-Crow	362
Woman	362
A Partisan's Protest	362
A Bequest to Music	363
Oneiromancy	363
July Fourth	363
A Paradox	364
Reedified	364
A Bulletin	364
An Inscription	365
An Erroneous Assumption	365
A Constructor	365
God Complies	366
In Articulo Mortis	366
The Discoverers	366
Unexpounded	366
The Eastern Question	367
Two Types	367
To a Critic of Tennyson	367

CONTENTS

	PAGE			PAGE
COOPERATION	368		FOR WOUNDS	372
HUMILITY	368		A LITERARY METHOD	372
STRAINED RELATIONS	368		BACK TO NATURE	373
EXONERATION	369		RUDOLPH BLOCK	373
AFTER PORTSMOUTH	369		BOYCOTT	373
A VOICE FROM PEKIN	369		TO HER	374
A PIOUS RITE	370		CREATION	374
JUSTICE	370		REBUKE	374
AT THE BEACH	370		PRAYER	375
AN INFRACTION OF THE RULES	371		THE LONG FEAR	375
CONVERSELY	371		AN INSPIRED PERFORMANCE	375
A WARNING	371		SEPULTURE	376
PSYCHOGRAPHS	372			

SHAPES OF CLAY

THE PASSING SHOW

I

I know not if it was a dream. I viewed
A city where the restless multitude,
   Between the eastern and the western deep
Had reared gigantic fabrics, strong and rude.

Colossal palaces crowned every height;
Towers from valleys climbed into the light;
   O'er dwellings at their feet, great golden domes
Hung in the blue, barbarically bright.

But now, new-glimmering to-east, the day
Touched the black masses with a grace of gray,
   Dim spires of temples to the nation's God
Studding high spaces of the wide survey.

Well did the roofs their solemn secret keep
Of life and death stayed by the truce of sleep,
   Yet whispered of an hour when sleepers wake,
The fool to hope afresh, the wise to weep.

The gardens greened upon the builded hills
Above the tethered thunders of the mills
    With sleeping wheels unstirred to service yet
By the tamed torrents and the quickened rills.

A hewn acclivity, reprieved a space,
Looked on the builder's blocks about his base
    And bared his wounded breast in sign to say:
" Strike! 'tis my destiny to lodge your race.

" 'Twas but a breath ago the mammoth browsed
Upon my slopes, and in my caves I housed
    Your shaggy fathers in their nakedness,
While on their foemen's offal they caroused."

Ships from afar afforested the bay.
Within their huge and chambered bodies lay
    The wealth of continents; and merrily sailed
The hardy argosies to far Cathay.

Beside the city of the living spread—
Strange fellowship!—the city of the dead;
    And much I wondered what its humble folk,
To see how bravely they were housed, had said.

Noting how firm their habitations stood,
Broad-based and free of perishable wood—
    How deep in granite and how high in brass
The names were wrought of eminent and good,

I said: "When gold or power is their aim,
The smile of beauty or the wage of shame,
 Men dwell in cities; to this place they fare
When they would conquer an abiding fame."

From the red East the sun—a solemn rite—
Crowned with a flame the cross upon a height
 Above the dead; and then with all his strength
Struck the great city all aroar with light!

II

I know not if it was a dream. I came
Unto a land where something seemed the same
 That I had known as 'twere but yesterday,
But what it was I could not rightly name.

It was a strange and melancholy land,
Silent and desolate. On either hand
 Lay waters of a sea that seemed as dead,
And dead above it seemed the hills to stand.

Grayed all with age, those lonely hills—ah me,
How worn and weary they appeared to be!
 Between their feet long dusty fissures clove
The plain in aimless windings to the sea.

One hill there was which, parted from the rest,
Stood where the eastern water curved a-west.
  Silent and passionless it stood. I thought
I saw a scar upon its giant breast.

The sun with sullen and portentous gleam
Hung like a menace on the sea's extreme;
  Nor the dead waters, nor the far, bleak bars
Of cloud were conscious of his failing beam.

It was a dismal and a dreadful sight,
That desert in its cold, uncanny light;
  No soul but I alone to mark the fear
And imminence of everlasting night!

All presages and prophecies of doom
Glimmered and babbled in the ghastly gloom,
  And in the midst of that accursèd scene
A wolf sat howling on a broken tomb.

ELIXIR VITÆ

Of life's elixir I had writ, when sleep
(Pray Heaven it spared him who the writing read!)
Settled upon my senses with so deep
A stupefaction that men thought me dead.
The centuries stole by with noiseless tread,

Like spectres in the twilight of my dream;
I saw mankind in dim procession sweep
Through life, oblivion at each extreme.
Meanwhile my beard, like Barbarossa's growing,
Loaded my lap and o'er my knees was flowing.

The generations came with dance and song,
And each observed me curiously there.
Some asked: "Who was he?" Others in the throng
Replied: "A wicked monk who slept at prayer."
Some said I was a saint, and some a bear—
These all were women. So the young and gay,
Visibly wrinkling as they fared along,
Doddered at last on failing limbs away;
Though some, their footing in my beard entangled,
Fell into its abysses and were strangled.

At last a generation came that walked
More slowly forward to the common tomb,
Then altogether stopped. The women talked
Excitedly; the men, with eyes agloom
Looked darkly on them with a look of doom;
And one cried out: "We are immortal now—
How need we these?" And a dread figure stalked,
Silent, with gleaming axe and shrouded brow,
And all men cried: "Decapitate the women,
Or soon there'll be no room to stand or swim in!"

So (in my dream) each lovely head was chopped
From its fair shoulders, and but men alone
Were left in all the world. Birth being stopped,
Enough of room remained in every zone,
And Peace ascended Woman's vacant throne.
Thus, life's elixir being found (the quacks
Their bread-and-butter in it gladly sopped)
'Twas made worth having by the headsman's axe.
Seeing which, I gave myself a hearty shaking,
And crumbled all to powder in the waking.

CONVALESCENT

What! " Out of danger?" Can the slighted **Dame**
Or canting Pharisee no more defame?
Will Treachery caress my hand no more,
Nor Hatred lie alurk about my door?—
Ingratitude, with benefits dismissed,
Not understanding what 'tis all about,
Will Envy henceforth not retaliate
For virtues it were vain to emulate?
Will Ignorance my knowledge fail to scout,
Not understanding what 'tis all about,
Yet feeling in its light so mean and small
That all his little soul is turned to gall?

What! " Out of danger?" Jealousy disarmed?
Greed from exaction magically charmed?

Ambition stayed from trampling whom it meets.
Like horses fugitive in crowded streets?
The Bigot, with his candle, book and bell,
Tongue-tied, unlunged and paralyzed as well?
The Critic righteously to justice haled,
His own ear to the post securely nailed—
What most he dreads unable to inflict,
And powerless to hawk the faults he's picked?
The Liar choked upon his choicest lie,
And impotent alike to vilify
Or flatter for the gold of thrifty men
Who hate his person but employ his pen—
Who love and loathe, respectively, the dirt
Belonging to his character and shirt?

What! "Out of danger?"—Nature's minions all,
Like hounds returning to the huntsman's call,
Obedient to the unwelcome note
That stays them from the quarry's bursting throat?—
Famine and Pestilence and Earthquake dire,
Torrent and Tempest, Lightning, Frost and Fire,
The soulless Tiger and the mindless Snake,
The noxious Insect from the stagnant lake,—
These from their immemorial prey restrained,
Their fury baffled and their power chained?
I'm safe? Is that what the physician said?
What! "Out of danger?" Then, by Heaven, I'm
    dead!

AT THE CLOSE OF THE CANVASS

'Twas a Venerable Person, whom I met one Sunday
   morning,
   All appareled as a prophet of a melancholy sect;
And in a Jeremiad of objurgatory warning
   He lifted up his *jodel* to the following effect:

" O ye sanguinary statesmen, intermit your verbal tussles!
   O ye editors and orators, consent to hear my lay!
Rest a little while the digital and maxillary muscles
   And attend to what a Venerable Person has to say.

" Cease your writing, cease your shouting, cease your
   wild unearthly lying;
   Cease to bandy such expressions as are never, never
   found
In the letter of a lover; cease "exposing" and "replying"
   Let there be abated fury and a decrement of sound.

" For to-morrow will be Monday and the fifth day of
   November—
   Only day of opportunity before the final rush.
Carpe diem! go conciliate each person who's a member
   Of the other party—do so while you can without a
   blush.

" Lo! the time is close upon you when the madness of
the season
Having howled itself to silence like a Minnesota
'clone,
Will at last be superseded by the still, small voice of
reason,
When the whelpage of your folly you would willingly
disown.

" Ah, 'tis mournful to consider what remorses will be
thronging,
With a consciousness of having been so ghastly indis-
creet,
When by accident untoward two ex-gentlemen belonging
To the opposite political denominations meet!

"Yes, 'tis melancholy, truly, to forecast the fierce, unruly
Supersurging of their blushes, like the flushes upon high
When Aurora Borealis lights her circumpolar palace
And in customary manner sets her banner in the sky.

" Each will think: ' This falsifier knows that I too am
a liar.
Curse him for a son of Satan, all unholily compound!
Curse my leader for another! Curse that pelican, my
mother!
Would to God that I when little in my victual had
been drowned! ' "

Then that venerable warner disappeared around a cor-
ner,
And the season of unreason having also taken flight,
All the cheeks of men were burning like the skies to
crimson turning
When Aurora Borealis fires her premises by night.

GEOTHEOS

As sweet as the look of a lover
  Saluting the eyes of a maid
  That blossom to blue as the maid
Is ablush to the glances above her,
  The sunshine is gilding the glade
  And lifting the lark out of shade.

Sing therefore high praises, and therefore
  Sing songs that are ancient as gold,
  Of earth in her garments of gold;
Nor ask of their meaning, nor wherefore
  They charm as of yore, for behold!
  The Earth is as fair as of old.

Sing songs of the pride of the mountains,
  And songs of the strength of the seas,
  And the fountains that fall to the seas

From the hands of the hills, and the fountains
  That shine in the temples of trees,
  In valleys of roses and bees.

Sing songs that are dreamy and tender,
  Of slender Arabian palms,
  And shadows that circle the palms,
Where caravans out of the splendor,
  Are kneeling in blossoms and balms,
  In islands of infinite calms.

Barbaric, O Man, was thy runing
  When mountains were stained as with wine
  By the dawning of Time, and as wine
Were the seas, yet its echoes are crooning,
  Achant in the gusty pine
  And the pulse of the poet's line.

POLITICS

That land full surely hastens to its end
Where public sycophants in homage bend
The populace to flatter, and repeat
The doubled echoes of its loud conceit.
Lowly their attitude but high their aim,
They creep to eminence through paths of shame,
Till, fixed securely in the seats of pow'r,
The dupes they flattered they at last devour.

THE VALLEY OF DRY BONES

With crow bones all the land is white,
From the gates of morn to the gates of night.
Picked clean, they lie on the cumbered ground,
And the politician's paunch is round;
And he strokes it down and across as he sings:
" I've eaten my fill of the legs and wings,
The neck, the back, the pontifical nose,
Breast, belly and gizzard, for everything goes.
The meat that's dark (and there's none that's white)
Exceeded the need of my appetite,
But I've bravely stuck to the needful work
That a hungry domestic hog would shirk.
I've eaten the fowl that the Fates commend
To reluctant lips of the People's Friend.
Rank unspeakably, bitter as gall,
Is the bird, but I've eaten it, feathers and all.
I'm a dutiful statesman, I am, although
I really *don't* like a diet of crow.
So I've dined all alone in a furtive way,
But my platter I've cleaned every blessed day.
They say that I bolt; so I do—my bird;
They say that I sulk, but they've widely erred!
O Lord! if my enemies only knew
How I'm full to the throat with the corvic stew

They'd open their ears to hear me profess
The faith compelled by the corvic stress,
(For, alas! necessity knows no law)
In the heavenly caucus—' Caw! Caw! Caw!'"

And that ornithanthropical person tried
By flapping his arms on the air to ride;
But I knew by the way that he clacked his bill
He was just the poor, featherless biped, Dave Hill.
   1896.

POLYPHEMUS

Twas a sick young man with a face ungay
   And an eye that was all alone;
And he shook his head in a hopeless way
   As he sat on a roadside stone.

" O, ailing youth, what untoward fate
   Has made the sun to set
On your mirth and eye?" " I'm constrained to
     state
   I'm an ex-West Point cadet.

" 'Twas at cannon-practice I got my hurt
   And my present frame of mind;
For the gun went off with a double spurt—
   Before it, and also behind!"

" How sad, how sad, that a fine young chap,
   When studying how to kill,
Should meet with so terrible a mishap
   Precluding eventual skill.

" Ah, woful to think that a weapon made
   For mowing down the foe
Should commit so dreadful an escapade
   As to turn about to mow ! "

No more he heeded while I condoled:
   He was wandering in his mind;
His lonely eye unconsidered rolled,
   And his views he thus defined:

" 'Twas O for a breach of the peace—'twas O
   For an international brawl!
But a piece of the breech—ah no, ah no,
   I didn't want that at all."

IN DEFENSE

You may say if you please, Johnny Bull, that our girls
Are crazy to marry your dukes and your earls;
But I've heard that the maids of your own little isle
Greet bachelor lords with a favoring smile.

Nay, titles, 'tis said in defense of our fair,
Are popular here because popular there;
And for them our ladies persistently go
Because 'tis exceedingly English, you know.

Whatever the motive, you'll have to confess
The effort's attended with easy success;
And—pardon the freedom—'tis thought, over here,
'Tis mortification you mask with a sneer.

It's all very well, sir, your scorn to parade
Of the high nasal twang of the Yankee maid,
But, ah, to my lord when he dares to propose
No sound is so sweet as that " Yes " from the nose.

Ah, well, if the dukes and the earls and that lot
Can stand it (God succor them if they can not!)
Your commoners ought to assent, I am sure,
And what they're not called on to suffer, endure.

" 'Tis nothing but money?—your nobles are bought "?
As to that, I submit, it is commonly thought
That England's a country not specially free
Of Crœsi and (if you'll allow it) Crœsæ.

You've many a widow and many a girl
With money to purchase a duke or an earl.

'Tis a very remarkable thing, you'll agree,
When goods import buyers from over the sea.

Alas for the woman of Albion's isle!
She may simper; as well as she can she may smile;
She may wear pantalettes and an air of repose—
But my lord of the future will talk through his nose.

INVOCATION

Read at the Celebration of Independence in San Francisco, in
1888.

Goddess of Liberty! O thou
    Whose tearless eyes behold the chain,
    And look unmoved upon the slain,
Eternal peace upon thy brow,—

Before thy shrine the races press,
    Thy perfect favor to implore—
    The proudest tyrant asks no more,
The ironed anarchist no less.

Thine altar-coals that touch the lips
    Of prophets kindle, too, the brand
    By Discord flung with wanton hand
Among the houses and the ships.

Upon thy tranquil front the star
  Burns bleak and passionless and white,
  Its cold inclemency of light
More dreadful than the shadows are.

Thy name we do not here invoke
  Our civic rites to sanctify:
  Enthroned in thy remoter sky,
Thou heedest not our broken yoke.

Thou carest not for such as we:
  Our millions die to serve the still
  And secret purpose of thy will.
They perish—what is that to thee?

The light that fills the patriot's tomb
  Is not of thee. The shining crown
  Compassionately offered down
To those who falter in the gloom,

And fall, and call upon thy name,
  And die desiring—'tis the sign
  Of a diviner love than thine,
Rewarding with a richer fame.

To him alone let freemen cry
  Who hears alike the victor's shout,

The song of faith, the moan of doubt,
And bends him from his nearer sky.

———

God of my country and my race!
  So greater than the gods of old—
  So fairer than the prophets told
Who dimly saw and feared thy face,—

Who didst but half reveal thy will
  And gracious ends to their desire,
  Behind the dawn's advancing fire
Thy tender day-beam veiling still,—

To whom the unceasing suns belong,
  And cause is one with consequence,—
  To whose divine, inclusive sense
The moan is blended with the song,—

Whose laws, imperfect and unjust,
  Thy just and perfect purpose serve:
  The needle, howsoe'er it swerve,
Still warranting the sailor's trust,—

God, lift thy hand and make us free
  To crown the work thou hast designed.
  O, strike away the chains that bind
Our souls to one idolatry!

The liberty thy love hath given
  We thank thee for. We thank thee for
  Our great dead fathers' holy war
Wherein our manacles were riven.

We thank thee for the stronger stroke
  Ourselves delivered and incurred
  When—thine incitement half unheard—
The chains we riveted we broke.

We thank thee that beyond the sea
  Thy people, growing ever wise,
  Turn to the west their serious eyes
And dumbly strive to be as we.

As when the sun's returning flame
  Upon the Nileside statue shone,
  And struck from the enchanted stone
The music of a mighty fame,

Let Man salute the rising day
  Of Liberty, but not adore.
  'Tis Opportunity—no more—
A useful, not a sacred, ray.

It bringeth good, it bringeth ill,
  As he possessing shall elect.

He maketh it of none effect
Who walketh not within thy will.

Give thou more or less, as we
    Shall serve the right or serve the wrong.
    Confirm our freedom but so long
As we are worthy to be free.

But when (O, distant be the time!)
    Majorities in passion draw
    Insurgent swords to murder Law,
And all the land is red with crime;

Or—nearer menace!—when the band
    Of feeble spirits cringe and plead
    To the gigantic strength of Greed,
And fawn upon his iron hand;—

Nay, when the steps to state are worn
    In hollows by the feet of thieves,
    And Mammon sits among the sheaves
And chuckles while the reapers mourn:

Then stay thy miracle!—replace
    The broken throne, repair the chain,
    Restore the interrupted reign
And veil again thy patient face.

Lo! here upon the world's extreme
　We stand with lifted arms and dare
　By thine eternal name to swear
Our country, which so fair we deem—

Upon whose hills, a bannered throng,
　The spirits of the sun display
　Their flashing lances day by day
And hear the sea's pacific song—

Shall be so ruled in right and grace
　That men shall say: " O, drive afield
　The lawless eagle from the shield,
And call an angel to the place! "

RELIGION

Hassan Bedreddin, clad in rags, ill-shod,
Sought the great temple of the living God.
　The worshipers arose and drove him forth,
And one in power beat him with a rod.

" Allah," he cried, " thou seest what I got:
Thy servants bar me from the sacred spot."
　" Be comforted," the Holy One replied;
" It is the only place where I am not."

TWO SOCIALISTS

Brand Whitlock sped from Hell through
    space,
  To be remanded never—
For having such a saintly face,
  Set free forever,

With due apology. He came
  To a world so base and bestial
No tongue infernal spake its name—
  No tongue celestial.

So foul it was that even He
  Had cast it off Who made it:
Adrift in space, as on a sea,
  No mooring stayed it.

That orb unclean, denied the aid
  Of gravitation's tether,
For centuries had blindly strayed—
  Lost altogether!

The sun disdainfully declined
  To light the villain planet,
And the whole universe combined
  To curse and ban it.

The Thief Impenitent, his grim
    Recusance unabated,
Was its sole occupant: for him
    It was created.

For when the wretch was newly dead
    'Twas thought Hell had not ample
Restraints to check the local spread
    Of his example,

Nor apparatus that insure'd
    A proper pang; though lately
The woes that he at first endured
    Had softened greatly.

But still one fierce, vain longing he
    Suffered, nor could o'ercome it—
The wish to sit in reverie
    On Calvary's summit.

Beneath that orb's unjoyous sky
    Brand Whitlock found the sinner.
Affinity!—the outer eye
    Lit by the inner.

Said Whitlock: "Here my stay is brief;
    Take, brother, ere we sever,

Thy pardon. Be a better thief
  Henceforth forever.

"God gives me power to condone
  All scalawags' offending,
For the sweet faith that I have shown
  In their amending."

When so he'd said with solemn grace
  As was that good soul's habit,
The Thief directly into space
  Sprang like a rabbit!

(He might have left at any time
  Had freedom been his passion,
For God had long forgot his crime.
  Crime was the fashion.)

The Saint, resuming soon his flight,
  Met him through chaos floating.
Three stolen post-holes that poor wight
  Was gaily toting.

A MORNING FANCY

I drifted (or I seemed to) in a boat
  Upon the surface of a shoreless sea
Whereon no ship nor anything did float,

Save only the frail bark supporting me;
And that—it was so shadowy—seemed to be
Almost from out the subtle azure wrought
Of the great ocean underneath its keel;
And all that blue profound appeared as naught
But thicker sky, translucent to reveal,
Miles down, whatever through its spaces glided,
Or at the bottom traveled or abided.

Great cities there I saw; of rich and poor
The palace and the hovel; mountains, vales,
Forest and field; the desert and the moor;
Tombs of the good and wise who'd lived in jails;
Seas of a denser fluid, white with sails
Pushed at by currents moving here and there
And sensible to sight above the flat
Of that opaquer deep.   Ah, strange and fair
The nether world that I was gazing at
With beating heart from that exalted level,
And, lest I founder, trembling like the devil!

The cities all were populous: men swarmed
In public places—chattered, laughed and wept;
And savages their shining bodies warmed
At fires in primal woods. The wild beast leapt
Upon its prey and slew it as it slept.
Armies went forth to battle on the plain

So far, far down in that unfathomed deep
The living seemed as silent as the slain,
Nor even the widows could be heard to weep.
One might have thought their shaking was but
laughter;
And, truly, most were married shortly after.

Above the wreckage of that silent fray
Strange fishes swam in circles, round and round—
Black, double-finned; and once a little way
A bubble rose and burst without a sound
And a man tumbled out upon the ground.
Lord! 'twas an eerie thing to drift apace
On that pellucid sea, beneath black skies
And o'er the heads of an undrowning race!
And when I woke I said—to her surprise
Who came with chocolate, for me to drink it:
" The atmosphere is deeper than you think it."

VISIONS OF SIN

Kraslajorsk, Siberia.—My eyes are better, and I shall travel
slowly toward home.—Danenhower.

From the regions of the Night,
Coming with recovered sight—
From the spell of darkness free,
What will Danenhower see?

He will see when he arrives
Doctors taking human lives.
He will see a learned judge
Whose decision will not budge
Till both litigants are fleeced
And his palm is duly greased.
Lawyers he will see who fight
Day by day and night by night;
Never both upon a side,
Though their fees they still divide.
Preachers he will see who teach
That it is divine to preach—
That they fan a sacred fire
And are worthy of their hire.
He will see a trusted wife,
Pride of some good husband's life,
Enter at a certain door
And—but he will see no more.
He will see Good Templars reel—
See a prosecutor steal,
And a father beat his child.
He'll perhaps see Oscar Wilde.

From the regions of the Night
Coming with recovered sight—
From the bliss of blindness free,
That's what Danenhower'll see.
  1882.

GENIUS

What is the thing called Genius? One has said
  'Tis general ability directed
Into a special channel. One, instead,
  Proffers a definition much respected
By toiling dullards: genius, he explains,
Is infinite capacity for taking pains.

Max Nordau, seeing he has not the thing,
  Has solemnly decided, with Lombroso,
That genius is degeneracy. Ring
  The curtain down—the show is only so-so;
I'd rather see a dog-fight than sit out
This inconclusive definition-bout.

What, then, is genius? Faith, I'm only sure
  That I am deep in doubt about the matter;
But this I *think:* of two in literature
  He is the greater genius who's the fatter.
'Twas in an age less prosperous that those
Were kings of thought who starved by verse and
    prose.

Lo! the lean rhapsodist whose soul surveys,
  Ecstatic, his unprofitable vision,
Interprets it in cleanly speech; arrays

His jeweled words with scholarly precision!
Faith, he's a dunce or he would never lack
The means to wedge his belly from his back.

'Twere passing easy to allay his pang
  Had he the genius—that's to say, the insight
Commercial. If he would but sing in slang
  He'd earn the wherewithal to make his skin tight.
Genius (let's now define the word afresh)
Is the capacity to take on flesh.

Spirit of Letters, hail! Thy reign is Now;
  Thy ministers are gentlemen that waddle—
Children of light and leading who avow
  They swap, for tallow, speech that's not a model,—
For laminated kidney-suet trade
Unsavory words. You must be stout, George Ade.

THE TOWN OF DÆ

Swains and maidens, young and old,
You to me this tale have told.

Where the squalid town of Dæ
Irks the comfortable sea,
Spreading webs to gather fish,
As for wealth we set a wish,

Dwelt a king by right divine,
Sprung from Adam's royal line.
 Town of Dæ by the sea,
  Divers kinds of kings there be.

Name nor fame had Picklepip:
Ne'er a soldier nor a ship
Bore his banners in the sun;
 Naught knew he of kingly sport,
 And he held his royal court
Under an inverted tun.
Love and roses, ages through,
 Bloom where cot and trellis stand;
Never yet these blossoms grew—
Never yet was room for two—
 In a cask upon the strand.
So it happened, as it ought,
That his simple schemes he wrought
Through the lagging summer's day
In a solitary way.
So it happened, as was best,
That he took his nightly rest
 With no dreadful weight of woe,
This way eyed and that way tressed,
 Featured thus, and thus, and so,
Lying lead-like on a breast
By cares of state enough oppressed.
Yet in dreams his fancy rude

Claimed a lordly latitude.
　Town of Dæ by the sea,
Dreamers mate above their state
　And waken back to their degree.

Once to cask himself away
He prepared at close of day.
As he tugged with swelling throat
At a most unkingly coat—
Not to get it off but on,
For the serving sun was gone—
Passed a silk-appareled sprite
Toward her castle on the height,
Seized and set the garment right.
Turned the startled Picklepip
Splendid crimson cheek and lip!
Turned again to sneak away,
But she bade the villain stay,
Bade him thank her, which he did
With a speech that slipped and slid,
Sprawled and stumbled in its gait
As a dancer tries to skate.
　Town of Dæ by the sea,
In the face of silk and lace
　Rags too bold should never be.

Lady Minnow cocked her head:
" Mister Picklepip," she said,

" Do you ever think to wed ? "
   Town of Dæ by the sea,
No fair lady ever made a
   Wicked speech like that to me!

Wretched little Picklepip
Said he hadn't any ship,
Any flocks at his command,
Nor to feed them any land;
Said he never in his life
Owned a mine to keep a wife.
But the guilty stammer so
That his meaning wouldn't flow;
So he thought his aim to reach
By some figurative speech:
Said his Fate had been unkind
Had pursued him from behind
   (How the mischief could it else?)
Came upon him unaware,
Caught him all too roughly—there
Gushed the little lady's glee
   Like a gush of golden bells:
" Picklepip, why, that is me!"
   Town of Dæ by the sea,
Grammar's for great scholars—she
   Loved the summer and the lea.

Stupid little Picklepip
Allowed the subtle hint to slip—
Maundered on about the ship
That he did not chance to own;
   Told this grievance o'er and o'er,
   Knowing that she knew before;
Told her how he dwelt alone.
Lady Minnow, for reply,
Cut him off with " So do I."
But she reddened at the fib;
Servitors had she, *ad lib.*
   Town of Dæ by the sea,
In her youth who speaks no truth
   Ne'er shall young and honest be.

Witless little Picklepip
Manned again his mental ship
And veered her with a sudden shift:
   Painted to the lady's thought
   How he wrestled and he wrought
Stoutly with the swimming drift
   By the kindly river brought
From the mountain to the sea,
Fuel for the town of Dæ.
Tedious tale for lady's ear:
   From her castle on the height,
   She had watched her water-knight
Through the seasons of a year

Challenge more than met his view
And conquer better than he knew.
Now she shook her pretty pate
And stamped her foot—'twas growing late:
" Mister Picklepip, when I
Drifting seaward pass you by;
When the waves my forehead kiss
   And my tresses float above—
   Dead and drowned for lack of love—
You'll be sorry, sir, for this! "
And the silly creature cried—
Feared, perchance, the rising tide.

   Town of Dæ by the sea,
Madam Adam, when she had 'em.
   May have been as bad as she.

Fiat lux!   Love's lumination
Fell in floods of revelation!
Blinded brain by world aglare,
Sense of pulses in the air,
Sense of swooning and the beating
Of a voice somewhere repeating
Something indistinctly heard!
   And the soul of Picklepip
   Sprang upon his trembling lip,
But he spake no further word
Of the wealth he did not own;
In that moment had outgrown

Ship and mine and flock and land—
Even his cask upon the strand.
Dropped a stricken star to earth,
Type of wealth and worldly worth.
Clomb the moon into the sky,
Type of love's immensity!
Shaking silver seemed the sea,
Throne of God the town of Dæ!
    Town of Dæ by the sea,
From above there cometh love,
    Blessing all good souls that be.

AN ANARCHIST

False to his art and to the high command
God laid upon him, Demagogo's hand
Beats all in vain the harp he thrilled before:
It yields a jingle and it yields no more.
No more the strings beneath his finger-tips
Sing harmonies divine. No more his lips,
Touched with a living coal from sacred fires,
Lead the sweet chorus of the golden wires.
The voice is raucous and the phrases squeak;
They labor, they complain, they sweat, they reek!
The more the wayward, disobedient song
Errs from the right to advocate the wrong,

More diligently still the singer strums,
To drown the horrid sound, with all his thumbs.
Gods, what a spectacle! The angels lean
Out of high Heaven to view the sorry scene,
And Israfel, "whose heart-strings are a lute,"
Though now compassion makes their music mute,
Among the weeping company appears,
Pearls in his eyes and cotton in his ears.

AN OFFER OF MARRIAGE

Once I " dipt into the future far as human eye could see,"
And saw—it was not Sandow, nor John Sullivan, but
  she—
Emancipated Woman, who was weeping as she ran
Here and there for the discovery of Expurgated Man.
But the sun of Evolution ever rose and ever set,
And that tardiest of mortals hadn't evolved yet.
Hence the tears that she cascaded, hence the sighs that
  tore apart
All the tendinous connections of her indurated heart.
Cried Emancipated Woman, as she wearied of the search:
" In Advancing I have left myself distinctly in the lurch!
Seeking still a worthy partner, from the land of brutes
  and dudes
I have penetrated rashly into manless solitudes.

Now without a mate of any kind where am I?—that's
    to say,
Where shall I be to-morrow?—where exert my rightful
    sway
And the purifying strength of my emancipated mind?
Can solitude be lifted up, vacuity refined?
Calling, calling from the shadows in the rear of my
    Advance—
From the region of Unprogress in the dark domain of
    Chance—
Long I heard the Unevolvable beseeching my return
To share the degradation he's reluctant to unlearn.
But I've held my way regardless, evoluting year by
    year
Till I'm what you now behold me—or would if you
    were here—
A condensed Emancipation and a Purifier proud,
An Independent Entity appropriately loud!
Independent? Yes, in spirit, but (O woful, woful
    state!)
Doomed to premature extinction by privation of a
    mate—
To extinction or reversion, for Unexpurgated Man
Still awaits me in the backward if I sicken of the van.
O the horrible dilemma!—to be odiously linked
With an Undeveloped Species, or become a Type Ex-
    tinct!"

As Emancipated Woman wailed her sorrow to the air,
Stalking out of desolation came a being strange and
    rare—
Plato's Man!—a biped, featherless from mandible to
    rump,
Its wings two quilless flippers and its tail a plumeless
    stump.
First it scratched and then it clucked, as if in hospitable
    terms
It invited her to banquet on imaginary worms.
Then it strutted up before her with a lifting of the head,
And in accents of affection and of sympathy it said:
" My estate is some'at 'umble, but I'm qualified to draw
Near the hymeneal altar and whack up my heart and
    claw
To Emancipated Anything as walks upon the earth;
And them things is at your service for whatever they are
    worth.
I'm sure to be congenial, marm, nor e'er deserve a
    scowl—
I'm Emancipated Rooster, I am Expurgated Fowl! "

From the future and its wonders I withdrew my gaze,
    and then
Wrote this wild, unfestive lay of Evolutionated Hen.

ARMA VIRUMQUE

"Ours is a Christian army"; so he said
A regiment of bangomen who led.
"And ours a Christian navy," added he
Who sailed a thunder-junk upon the sea.
Better they know than men unwarlike do
What is an army, and a navy too.
Pray God there may be sent them by-and-by
The knowledge what a Christian is, and why.
For somewhat lamely the conception runs
Of a brass-buttoned Jesus firing guns.

ON A PROPOSED CREMATORY

When a fair bridge is builded o'er the gulf
Between two cities, some ambitious fool,
Hot for distinction, pleads for earliest leave
To push his clumsy feet upon the span,
That men in after years may single him,
Saying: "Behold the fool who first went o'er!"
So be it when, as now the promise is,
Next summer sees the edifice complete

Which some do name a crematorium,
Within the vantage of whose greater maw's
Quicker digestion we shall cheat the worm
And circumvent the handed mole who loves,
With tunnel, adit, drift and roomy stope,
To mine our mortal parts in all their dips
And spurs and angles. Let the fool stand forth
To link his name with this fair enterprise,
As first decarcassed by the flame. And if
With rival greedings for the fiery fame
They push in clamoring multitudes, or if
With unaccustomed modesty they all
Hold off, being something loth to qualify,
Let me select the fittest for the rite.
By Heaven! I'll make so warrantable, wise
And excellent censure of their true deserts,
And such a searching canvass of their claims,
That none shall bait the allot. I'll spread my
      choice
Upon the main and general of those
Who, moved of holy impulse, pulpit-born,
Protested 'twere a sacrilege to burn
God's gracious images, designed to rot—
Who bellowed for the right of way for each
Distempered carrion through the water pipes.
With such a sturdy, boisterous exclaim
They did discharge themselves from their own
      throats

Against the splintered gates of audience
'Twere wholesomer to take them in at mouth
Than ear. These shall burn first: their ignoble
And seasoned substances—trunks, legs and arms,
Blent indistinguishable in a mass,
Like winter-woven serpents in a pit,
None vantaged with unfair precedency
And all impartially alive—shall serve
As fueling to fervor the retort
For after cineration of true men.

A DEMAND

You promised to paint me a picture,
    Dear Mat,
  And I was to pay you in rhyme.
Although I am loth to inflict your
  Most easy of consciences, I'm
Of opinion that fibbing is awful,
And breaking a contract unlawful,
  Indictable, too, as a crime,
    A slight and all that.

If, Lady Unbountiful, any
    Of that
  By mortals called pity has part

In your obdurate soul—if a penny
    You care for the health of my heart,
By performing your undertaking
You'll succor that organ from breaking—
    And spare it for some new smart,
        As puss does a rat.

Do you think it is very becoming,
        Dear Mat,
    To deny me my rights evermore?
And—bless you! if I begin summing
    Your sins they will make a long score!
You never were generous, madam:
If you had been Eve and I Adam
    You'd have given me naught but the core,
        And little of that.

Had I been content with a Titian,
        A cat
    By Landseer, a meadow by Claude,
No doubt I'd have had your permission
    To take it—by purchase abroad.
But why should I sail o'er the ocean
For Landseers and Claudes? I've a notion
    All's bad that the critics belaud.
        I wanted a Mat.

Presumption's a sin, and I suffer
    For that:
But still you *did* say that sometime,
If I'd pay you enough (here's enougher—
    That's more than enough) of rhyme
You'd paint me a picture.   I pay you
Hereby in advance; and I pray you
    Condone, while you can, your crime,
        And send me a Mat.

But if you don't do so I warn you,
    Dear Mat,
    I'll raise such a clamor and cry
On Parnassus the Muses will scorn you
    As mocker of poets and fly
With bitter complaints to Apollo:
" Her spirit is proud, her heart hollow,
    Her beauty "—they'll hardly deny,
        On second thought, *that!*

THE WEATHER-WIGHT

The way was long, the hill was steep,
My footing scarcely I could keep.

The night enshrouded me in gloom,
I heard the ocean's distant boom—

The trampling of the surges vast
Was borne upon the rising blast.

"God help the mariner," I cried,
"Whose ship to-morrow braves the tide!"

Then from the impenetrable dark
A solemn voice made this remark:

"For this locality—warm, bright;
Barometer unchanged; breeze light."

"Unseen consoler-man," I cried,
"Whoe'er you are, where'er abide,

"Thanks—but my care is somewhat less
For Jack's, than for my own, distress.

"Could I but find a friendly roof,
Small odds what weather were aloof.

"For he whose comfort is secure
Another's pain can well endure."

"The latch-string's out," the voice replied,
"And so's the door—jes' step inside."

Then through the darkness I discerned
A hovel into which I turned.

Groping about beneath its thatch,
I struck my head and then a match.

A candle by that gleam betrayed
Soon lent paraffinaceous aid.

A pallid, bald and thin old man
I saw, who this complaint began:

" Through summer suns and winter snows
I sets observin' of my toes.

" I rambles with increasin' pain
The path of duty, but in vain.

" Rewards and honors pass me by—
No Congress hears this raven cry! "

Filled with astonishment, I spoke:
" Thou ancient raven, why this croak?

" With observation of your toes
What Congress has to do, God knows!

"And swallow me if e'er I knew
That one could sit and ramble too!"

To answer me that ancient swain
Took up his parable again:

"Through winter snows and summer suns
A Weather Bureau here I runs.

"I calls the turn, and can declare
Jes' when she'll storm and when she'll fair.

"Three times a day I sings out clear
The probs to all which wants to hear.

"Some weather stations, run with light
Frivolity, is seldom right.

"A scientist from times remote,
In Scienceville my birth is wrote.

"And when I h'ist the 'rainy' sign
Jes' take your clo'es in off the line."

"Not mine, O marvelous old man,
The methods of your art to scan,

"Yet here no instruments there be—
Nor 'ometer nor 'scope I see.

"Did you (if questions you permit)
At the asylum leave your kit?"

That strange old man with motion rude
Rose to surprising altitude.

"Tools (and sarcazzems too) I scorns—
I tells the weather by my corns.

"No doors and windows here you see—
The wind and m'isture enters free.

"No fires nor lights, no wool nor fur
Here falsifies the tempercher.

"My corns unleathered I expose
To feel the rain's foretellin' throes.

"No stockin' from their ears keeps out
The comin' tempest's warnin' shout.

"Sech delicacy some has got
They know next summer's to be hot.

" This here one says (for that he's best) :
' Storm center passin' to the west.'

" This feller's vitals is transfixed
With frost for Janawary sixt'.

" One chap jes' now is occypied
In fig'rin on next Fridy's tide.

" I've shaved this cuss so thin and true
He'll spot a fog in South Peru.

" Sech are my tools, which ne'er a swell
Observatory can excel.

" By long a-studyin' their throbs
I catches onto all the probs."

Much more, no doubt, he would have said,
But suddenly he turned and fled ;

For in mine eye's indignant green
Lay storms that he had not foreseen,

Concerning which, as Fear appeals
To Speed, his toes had told his heels.

T. A. H.

Yes, he was that, or that, as you prefer—
Did so and so, though, faith, it wasn't all;
Lived like a fool, or a philosopher,
And had whatever's needful to a fall.
As rough inflections on a planet merge
In the true bend of the gigantic sphere,
Nor mar the perfect circle of its verge,
So in the survey of his worth the small
Asperities of spirit disappear,
Lost in the grander curves of character.
He lately was hit hard: none knew but I
The strength and terror of that ghastly stroke—
Not even herself. He uttered not a cry,
But set his teeth and made a revelry;
Drank like a devil—straining sometimes red
The goblet's edge; diced with his conscience; spread,
Like Sisyphus, a feast for Death and spoke
His welcome in a tongue so long forgot
That even his ancient guest remembered not
What race had cursed him in it. Thus my friend,
Still conjugating with each failing sense
The verb " to die " in every mood and tense,
Pursued his awful humor to the end.
When like a stormy dawn the crimson broke
From his white lips he smiled and mutely bled,
And, having meanly lived, is grandly dead.

MY MONUMENT

It is pleasant to think, as I'm watching my ink
   A-drying along my paper,
That a monument fine will surely be mine
   When death has extinguished my taper.

From each pitiless scribe of the critic tribe
   Purged clean of all sentiments narrow,
A pebble will mark his respect for the stark
   Stiff body that's under the barrow.

Thus stone upon stone by reviewers thrown,
   Will make my celebrity deathless.
O I wish I could think, as I gaze at my ink,
   They'd wait till my carcass is breathless.

MAD

   O ye who push and fight
     To hear a wanton sing—
   Who utter the delight
     That has the bogus ring,—

   O men mature in years,
     In understanding young,
   The membranes of whose ears
     She tickles with her tongue,—

O wives and daughters sweet,
  Who call it love of art
To kiss a woman's feet
  That crush a woman's heart,—

O prudent dams and sires,
  Your docile young who bring
To see how man admires
  A sinner if she sing—

O husbands who impart
  To each assenting spouse
The lesson that shall start
  The buds upon your brows,—

All whose applauding hands
  Assist to rear the flame
That throws o'er all the lands
  The shadow of its shame,—

Go drag her car!—the mud
  Through which its axle rolls
Is partly human blood
  And partly human souls.

Mad, mad!—your senses whirl
  Like devils dancing free

Because a strolling girl
Can hold the note high C.

For this the avenging rod
Of Heaven ye dare defy,
And tear the law that God
Thundered from Sinai!

FOR COERCION OF COLOMBIA

" The ships steam south
From the harbor mouth
    In warlike, grim array!
They load the seas,
And on every breeze
    I hear the brass bands play
    As the squadrons steer away.

"From each foreign shore
They are coming o'er
    The oceans big and small,
With cheering crews
And churning screws,
    And guns and shot and all,
    And Admirals that appal!

" In tropical seas
They are thick as bees.
   Oh, ne'er on the Trojan strand
Was gathered a fleet
So hard to beat
   As sails to that southern land.
   'Tis terribly, terribly grand!

" O sailorman stout,
What's it all about?
   If you happen to know tell me.
That the foe has no chance
His troops to advance
   To the field we all agree,
   And the devil a ship has he."

He shifted his quid,
The sailorman did,
   To the starboard side of his face.
His trousers he hitched
As he rolled and pitched,
   Maintaining his dubious place
   With a certain maritime grace.

He looked at the sky
With a studious eye,
   And this singular yarn he spun:

" When the wind's sou'west
Every man's possessed
　Of a devil!—no son-of-a-gun
　Can tell what's fit to be done."

Perhaps it was naught
But a sailorman's thought,
　But I said to myself: "I'm blest
If I can't mark down
A man of renown
　Who is living in mental unrest
　Where the wind is forever sou'west."

A TEAGOING ADMIRAL

Once the Queen of Nether China
(So benign a Messalina!)
Said: " I'll make a Naval Hero
Without fear—O brave as Nero!
He shall dominate the ocean
By promotion, that's my notion.
All my other sons of thunder
Then shall plunder vainly under
This Incomparable Person,
Interspersin' lively cursin'
With their futile strife to shiver
Every river-pirate's liver,

And to ascertain the measure
Of his treasure at their leisure.
For I'll so arrange the looting
And the shooting and the hooting,
And the making frightful faces
(These grimaces are the bases
 Of our tactics) that they never,
Howsoever brave and clever,
Shall have any kind of inning
In the skinning now beginning.
And I'll see that in the story
Of the gory game of glory
The historian shall slight 'em
Or indict 'em—maybe bite 'em.
But the Hero of my making,
Whom I'm aching to be waking
Into visible existence,
He shall distance these Philistines.
Fame's loud trumpet—he shall hear it.
Blown with spirit in his ear, it
Shall extol his birth and breeding,
His exceeding knack at leading
In a sanguinary sea fight,
Or a tea fight, or a flea fight,
Till he burst with admiration
Of his station in the nation!
Then while all the people mock him,
I'll unfrock him! That will shock him."

Thus the Queen of Nether China,
The Regina Mun-Kee-Shina,
Made to Naval Evolution
A Confucian contribution.
    1898.

THE WOOER

In Ballybazoo the young men woo
With the irresistible hob-nail shoe;
But in Ghargharoo lived a maiden who
Was pleased to remark that it wouldn't do.

From Ghargharoo to Ballybazoo
This sternly dissenting maiden (who,
Etc.) went to reside—a lass
With a cheek of steel and a brow of brass.

Then all the young men of Ballybazoo
Took turns in calling early to woo
(With the irresistible hob-nail shoe)
The beautiful maiden from Ghargharoo.

As each fond lover with ardor threw
His heel in her upturned face there flew
A rain of sparks that consumed his eyes,
Affecting his mind with a great surprise.

When all the young men had renounced
  their sight,
The metal-faced maiden she sat upright,
Remarking: "There's nothing here to do—
A dull, dull village is Ballybazoo."

From Ballybazoo to Ghargharoo
The cheek-whole maiden her armament drew,
And her playmate lovers raised a hurroo
That saddened the sightless in Ballybazoo.

A stranger there was who cherished a heel
Of double-case-hardened, cold-rolled chrome
  steel!
And taking thought he decided to woo,
As 'twas his undoubted right to do.

To display his charms he removed his shoe,
And boarding her visage, began to woo.
And there in the gloaming, and not in vain,
The old, old story was told again.

It was long ago in the sainted past,
But traits long latent crop out at last;
And I know a live newspaper fellow who
Has ancestors buried in Ghargharoo.

SILHOUETTES OF ORIENTALS

The Sultan is a Muscleman;
  He's full of vim and whack,
And if you want a tussle man
  His back.

Because he's a Mahometan,
  They think him mighty slow.
He's quicker than a comet—an
  Auto!

He doesn't often waste a fit,
  But throws it where 'twill tell.
Blood? Yes, he likes the taste of it
  Right well.

That angel, the Bulgarian,
  Is just a bird of pray.
His soul's as white as Parian,
  They say.

His halo fits him pleasantly
  And he has two great wings.
He tunes his harp, and presently
  He sings:

" My shoulder inoffensively
　　Bears this dear little chip.
Pass on, wayfarer, pensively—
　　Don't flip."

The thoughtful Moslem pins the chip
　　Fast with a dagger. Oh,
That angel-person's sins of lip
　　Are low!

The Armenian is a sassy cur,
　　Cantankerous to boot,
Nor draws the line at massacre
　　And loot.

But when the Kurd in revelry
　　Slays, burns, imprisons, fines,
That bad gent to the devil he
　　Consigns.

My muse cannot exemplify
　　The Macedonian—she
Refuses to attempt to fly
　　So free.

Old Philip, King of Macedon,
　　Is many ages dead;

We have this little gassy don
Instead.

Is he a Unitarian,
  A Moslem, Buddhist, Jew—
Or just a gowned barbarian
With trousers on his Mary Ann?
  Don't know—do you?

LAND OF THE PILGRIMS' PRIDE

I dreamed, and in my dream came one who said:
" Because thou art all sullen; and because
Thou sayest thou hast not for thy country, love;
Because thou dost begrudge the foolish blood
That in the far heroic days thou didst
(Or sayst thou didst) pour from thy riven vein
In testimony to thy patriot zeal;
Because thou seekest ever to promote
Distrust of the benign and wholesome rule
Of the Majority—God's Ministers;
Because thou hearest in the People's voice
Naught but the mandate of an idiot will
Clamoring in the wilderness, but what
Or why it knoweth not; because all this
And much beside is true, I come——"

"Forbear," I cried, "to name thine errand—all
Too well I know it for the sword, the scales,
The shrouded eyes (albeit methinks I catch
A twinkle now and then beneath the band)
Speak to my conscience of a traitor's doom!
Strike, then, but hear. To westward, roaring up
From far beyond the earth's vast curvature,
Come sounds of discord horrible—the jar
And thunder of exploding bombs;
The crackle of the flames that eat away
The means of life of those who kindle them;
The shouts and curses of the robber mob,
Drunk with a sense of numbers—like the wolves,
Numerically brave—on ravin bent
And murder! Hear the moans of honest men,
With shameful by-name vilified, denied
The right to earn their bread, and with a blind,
Mad cruelty the devil would weep to see,
Beaten and tortured, even by the hands
Of the barbarian's female and his whelps!
Meanwhile the coward rulers of the land
Prate of 'the People's wrongs.' The coward press
(Thrifty withal to purse a double gain
By two-faced flattery) prates like a fool
Of the conservative and saving strength
Of Anglo-Saxon institutions, or
With magic words, as 'freedom,' and the like,
Would conjure order from inharmony.

The land is foul with crime, and none declares
Our shame and downfall. Even the women rise
And seeing the rack and ruin men have wrought,
Strip their weak bodies with a silly zeal
Something to save from the chaotic wreck;
And in the reek and sweat of their absurd
And awkward efforts, lose even what remained—
Their own morality and men's respect.
Therefore I say to you—"

                     " Nay say no more,"
Cried she who came into my dream, " for thou
Dost wander. What, pray, has all this to do
With what thou'rt charged with?—that thou dost
    not love—
Such as it is—thy country? "

                        Faith, I would,
But 'tis infested by my countrymen! "
What she replied I know not, for a bomb,
Spitting and sputtering on my chamber floor,
Awoke me and I fled into the night.

A SINGLE TERMER

When Senator Foraker came to die
   His features lit up with a glow,
And he said: " I am going to dwell on high
   And the Democrats down below.

"I have kept the faith, I have fought the fight,
  To the Trusts forever true.
With Elkins to lead, I have followed the light—
  Saint Peter, it's up to you."

Said Peter: "We strive to please in vain;
  Many a soul coming here
Escapes to earth to be born again
  And resume the old career."

Here he opened the gate. "Although, no doubt,
  This fellow's a son of sin,
The devil himself can't keep him out,
  But I'll lock the fine gentleman in."

A PLAGUE OF ASSES

Alas, we've fallen upon an evil time,
Our journals are all in a rash of rhyme.
Slang, "dialect," the humor of the slum,
Done into stanzas by the rule of thumb,
The peasant word, the coarse, colloquial phrase,
Fitting the pauper thought that it conveys,
March to the meter-master's "hep, hep, hep,"
With every second soldier out of step.
What sins of ours deserve this heavy curse?
Who taught our clowns 'tis easy to write verse

If neither poetry nor wit be deemed
A needful ornament, nor sense esteemed
A twin of sound? O rustics of the quill,
Ill-made by Nature, making others ill,
(Landlubbers on the sea of song a-sail
Uttering your fancies o'er the leeward rail)
Forgive the wicked wish I cannot choose
But entertain—that, luckless, you may lose
Each one a thumb of the tormenting ten
Whereon you reckon syllables. Ah, then,
Restored to what it was before you learned
That grinning through horse-collars ever earned
Plaudits of rustics and enough of dollars
To pay the weekly rental of the collars,
With something over for the stomach's throes,
Your ailing verse will turn to ailing prose.
Then joyous angels will look down and say:
"Behold! the ninety-nine that went astray
Return to where, from fields of noxious grass,
Sweet thistles beckon each repenting ass."

IN CUBA

Our Administration
Had made a new nation—
    As new as a nation could be.

A raven was flapping
Above it and snapping
  His beak with a manifest glee.
  " O raven, what is it you see
  That causes the manifest glee?

" You can't be designing
A programme of dining
  On anything living and free.
You're famous for dinners
That plain-speaking sinners
  Condemn with the Terrible D!
  (The word is abhorrent to me
  That begins with the Terrible D.)

" Come down from your airy
Position and tarry
  Awhile on this cocoanut tree,
And tell me what joying
You find in annoying
  A nation so young and so free—
  Not dead in the slightest degree,
  But lively and healthy as we."

The raven, complying,
Said, solemnly eying
  My edible parts from the tree:

" It isn't to nations
I look for my rations
 To any extent or degree.
 They don't fill the hollow in me
 To an appreciable degree.

" Yet the seasons ensuing
Will see something doing
 To heighten my manifest glee.
'Tis soldiers that mostly
Appeal to my ghostly
 Unusual appetite, see?
 They're easy digesting to me
 With my singular appetite, see?"

Then I hammered my forehead
To think of that horrid
 Old bird with his appetite free,
A-sitting there, lacking
Compassion and cracking
 His beak, on a cocoanut tree,
 As if merely saying to me:
 " Oh, what a fine cocoanut tree."

I said somewhat later:
" Our Administrator
Of Freedom's estate, O see!

His Administration
Presents us a ' nation '
   That's spelled with the Terrible D!
   And ' nation ' is hateful to me
   When led by the Terrible D."

FOR A CERTAIN CRITIC

Let lowly theme engage my humble pen—
Stupidities of critics, not of men.
Be it mine once more the maunderings to trace
Of the expounders' self-directed race—
Their wire-drawn fancies, finically fine,
Of diligent vacuity the sign.
Let them in jargon of their trade rehearse
The moral meaning of the random verse
That runs spontaneous from the poet's pen
To be half-blotted by ambitious men
Who hope with his their meaner names to link
By writing o'er it in another ink
The thoughts unreal which they think they think,
Until the mental eye in vain inspects
The hateful palimpsest to find the text.

The lark, ascending heavenward, loud and long
Sings to the dawning day his wanton song.

The moaning dove, attentive to the sound,
Its hidden meaning hastens to expound:
Explains its principles, design—in brief,
Pronounces it a parable of grief!
The bee, just pausing ere he daubs his thigh
With pollen from a hollyhock near by,
Declares he never heard in terms so just
The labor problem thoughtfully discussed!
The browsing ass looks up and clears his whistle
To say: " A monologue upon the thistle! "
Meanwhile the lark, descending, folds his wing
And innocently asks: "What!—did I sing? "

O literary parasites! who thrive
Upon the fame of better men, derive
Your sustenance by suction, like a leech,
And, for you preach of them, think masters preach,—
Who find it half is profit, half delight,
To write about what you could never write,—
Consider, pray, how sharp had been the throes
Of famine and discomfiture in those
You write of if they had been critics, too,
And doomed to write of nothing but of you!

Lo! where the gaping crowd throngs yonder tent,
To see the lion resolutely bent!

The prosing showman who the beast displays
Grows rich and richer daily in its praise.
But how if, to attract the curious yeoman,
The lion owned the show and showed the showman?

ARTHUR McEWEN

Posterity with all its eyes
Will come and view him where he lies.
Then, turning from the scene away
With a concerted shrug, will say:
"H'm, *Scarbæus Sisyphus*—
What interest has that to us?
We can't admire at all, at all,
A tumble-bug without its ball."
And then a sage will rise and say:
"Good friends, you err—turn back, I pray:
This freak that you unwisely shun
Is bug and ball rolled into one."

CHARLES AND PETER

Ere Gabriel's note to silence died
All graves of men were gaping wide.

Then Charles A. Dana, of *The Sun*
Rose slowly from the deepest one.

"The dead in Christ rise first, 'tis writ,"
Quoth he—"ick, bick, ban, doe,—I'm It!"

(His headstone, footstone, counted slow,
Were "ick" and "bick," he "ban" and "doe":

Of beating Nick the subtle art
Was part of his immortal part.)

Then straight to Heaven he took his flight,
Arriving at the Gates of Light.

There Warden Peter, in the throes
Of sleep, lay roaring in the nose.

"Get up, you sluggard!" Dana cried—
"I've an engagement there inside."

The Saint arose and scratched his head.
"I recollect your face," he said,

"(And, pardon me, 'tis rather hard)
But——" Dana handed him a card.

"Ah, yes, I now remember—bless
My soul, how dull I am!—yes, yes,

"Walk in. But I must tell you this:
We've nothing better here than bliss.

"We've rest and comfort, though, and peace."
"H'm—puddles," Dana said, " for geese.

"Have you in Heaven no Hell?"   "Why no,"
Said Peter, "nor, in truth, below.

"'Tis not included in our scheme—
'Tis but a preacher's idle dream."

The great man slowly moved away.
"I'll call," he said, "another day.

"On earth I played it, o'er and o'er,
And Heaven without it were a bore."

"O, stuff!—come in. You'll make," said Pete,
"A Hell where'er you set your feet."

CONTEMPLATION

I muse upon the distant town
    In many a dreamy mood.
Above my head the sunbeams crown
    The graveyard's giant rood.

The lupin blooms among the tombs,
The quail recalls her brood.

Ah, good it is to sit and trace
The shadow of the cross;
It moves so still from place to place
O'er marble, bronze and moss;
With graves to mark upon its arc
Our time's eternal loss.

And sweet it is to watch the bee
That revels in the roses,
And sense the fragrance floating free
On every breeze that dozes
Upon the mound, where, safe and sound,
Mine enemy reposes.

THE GOLDEN AGE

Long ago the world was finer—
Why it failed I do not know:
All the virtues were diviner;
Robber, miser, and maligner
Had not been created. No,
Truth and honor flourished, though,
Long ago.

Sages in procession stalking
  Moved majestic to and fro,
And each lowly mortal walking
In their shadow stilled his talking,
  Heeding the sonorous flow
  Of their wisdom, loud or low,
      Long ago.

Angel Woman, younger, fairer
  Far than she that now we know,
Gave men meeting with a rarer
Grace. No graybeard cried, " Beware her
  Tongue and temper! " She was slow
  To wrath. I tell you that was so,
      Long ago.

Ah, the miracle of morning,
  Setting all the world aglow
Like a smile of light adorning
God's own face, held no forewarning
  Of the tempest that would blow—
  Sign and prophecy of woe,
      Long ago.

Hope from every hilltop beckoned
  To the happy throngs below;
And they confidently reckoned

On a hero every second.
   Best of all that goodly show,
   I was but a laddie—O,
         So long ago!

A PROPHET OF PEACE

" The world is young, perverse, and bad,
   The virtues all are wanting;
The gods are dead and men are mad
   And wickedness is haunting
The human heart, an honored guest,
As robbers of the night infest
   A wayside inn in Camilhad.

" Hate walks the earth all unafraid,
   And neighbor murders neighbor;
Greed draws on Greed the battle-blade,
   And Labor strangles Labor.
The widow and the orphan cry
For bread while benefactors ply
   Unlashed by law, their dreadful trade.

" King, president, and patriot
   Serve their accurst ambition;
The soldier and the *sans-culottes,*
   The priest and politician,

Are blowing with impested breath
The coals of war that sparkle death.
   Peace, righteousness, and love are not.

"But I shall live to see the day
   Whose golden dawn is breaking!
The reign of war no more shall lay
   Our dust, nor hearts be aching.
Lo! all mankind in brotherhood
Shall study only to be good,
   And fling the sword of self away!"

So chanted one inspired and fain
   His message to deliver
To men who toiled upon the plain
   And bled along the river,
And all the world was foul with crime!
This prophet lived about the time
   That Lamech's wife bare Tubal-cain.

AN UNREFORMABLE REFORMER

I know not how they come about—
   These alterations in our spelling,
But sometimes am disposed to doubt
   The efficacy of compelling

(As still is done to one in school
  By threatening to whack or twist him)
Observance of an iron rule
  Despite one's better private system.
For when the sinner's freed from fear
He spells, as formerly, by ear.

That's what I have observed, but much
  By that, I fear, is not decided
Against the iron hand (whose touch
  May none experience, as I did)
For under this White House régime
  Condemning every silent letter,
This is the motto, it would seem:
  " Who spells by ear spells all the better."
If that is what these pranks entail,
Executive Compulsion, hail!

God grant I know not envy nor,
  When chatting over cup and saucer,
Betray my secret hunger for
  The high renown of Geoffrey Chaucer.
Yet now at last I seem to see
  My way to equal approbation:
When I'm as hard to read as he
  Phonetes of that far generation
Will study me and say: " How grand!—
So difficult to understand! "

The President, the President!--
  How enterprising in revision
Of Nature's laws!—how diligent
  In cutting out a court decision!—
How sedulous the stars to woo
  And keep the seasons rightly going!
Ah, seldom we remember who
  Establishes the time of sowing
And reaping, makes the harvest good,
And a great man of Leonard Wood.

This world is variously bad,
  And mad as hares in January
('Tis later that the hares are mad,
  But similes and seasons vary)
And Presidents have much to do
  To keep the March of Mind a-walking,
To level up the birth rate, to
  Pain William Chandler—all by talking.
O Father Adam, how you must
Rejoice that both your ears are dust!

THE WORD-WAY IN PANAMA

I dreamed I sailed along a tropic shore,
The Line behind me and the Star before.
A savage coast, it was, of wood and fen,
And monkeys gabbled there, instead of men.

Once, as the blessed sun his head upraised,
On what a wondrous spectacle he gazed!

A mile away upon the starboard beam
Fell into ocean a deep sluggish stream,
Yet not a drop of water passed its mouth—
Thy way, Kentucky, glory of the South!
Words, words alone it "uttered to the day,"
As if from Kansas it had gone astray.
Yea, disemboguing grandly on the beach,
Flowed thickly, viscidly, the parts of speech!
Some, by their dead, incalculable weight
Held to the bottom of that turbid strait,
Slid seaward fathoms deep, nor saw the light
That shone above their everlasting night!
Some, such their levity, remained atop,
Frolicked and flashed—did everything but stop.
Others, too grave to float, too light to sink,
Forever rolled and tumbled on the brink—
Spread north and south along the cumbered strand,
And babbled ever between sea and land.

Ah! 'twas a famous spectacle indeed,
This wordy welter!—verbs that disagreed
With nominatives; prepositions all
Too weak to hold the objective case in thrall;
Adverbs and adjectives disparted quite
From parent-words and in a woful plight

Of orphanage; conjunctions, interjections
With truly anarchistic predilections;
And pronouns which—a gutter-blooded swarm!—
Denied their antecedents in their form!

Greatly I marveled whence this language came—
No "well of English" like it could I name,
Nor think how such a stream, however free
Its flow, could wear a channel to the sea!

As Hudson bears his never-failing fleet
Of dead dogs, verdant, poddy and unsweet,
To pile themselves upon the Jersey shore,
Or in Sargasso's Sea rest evermore,
So poured this torrent through its delta's breaches,
And all these parts of speech were parts of speeches!—
All gushing from that word-way like a flood
Of swearing tomcats militant in mud!
They leapt, they smelled, they clamored, like a line
Of pagans faring to a sacred shrine!
"No more my heart the dismal din sustained"
(See Homer—Pope's translation) for it strained
My senses—this uncouth, infragrant, hoarse
"Fine flow of language" from its Northern source.
Cold drops of terror from my body broke!—
I 'bouted ship, and from my dream awoke.

1902.

THE JACK OF CLUBS

Jerome, you are a mighty famous man—
   District Attorney, I believe they call you.
Some shout your praise as loudly as they can,
   And some, apparently, just live to maul you.
   But whether good or ill repute befall you,
Your critics can't deny that, as a rule,
   You take it standing—though the wits among
Them say you stand, as does the singing mule,
   The better to perform your feats of lung.
And, truly from the dawning to the gloaming,
When in good voice, you're usually Jeroming.

O, well, we must have music—'tis a need,
   Like Ibsen, Shaw or the " Edenic diet ";
Though sometimes silence is desired—indeed,
   There's much that may be said in praise of quiet,
   And possibly you might do worse than try it.
'Twere better, anyhow, than fool advice
   To the police to club their fellow men,
Too sore already.   Sir, it is not nice
   To free your snouty virtues from the pen—
Unless, as once in Gadara, they'll scamper
Down a steep place to where 'tis greatly damper.

Jerome, the best of us are those who care
  To hide from view the monsters that inhabit
Our hearts, and when too closely questioned swear
  We've nothing fiercer than a sheep or rabbit.
  Seeing an opportunity, you grab it
And lifting up the curtain, show the whole
  Menagerie of thoughts and feelings which
Infest the secret places of your soul
  Like newts and water-puppies in a ditch.
O, great reformer! hide from observation
The unpleasing spectacle of Reformation.
  1905.

A NAVAL METHOD

  Captain Purvis, for aught *we* know,
  Never slew a Filipino;
  Played exceeding well at polo,
  But invited not the bolo.
  Though his form was big and burly,
  And his fist was hard and knurly,
  And his cocktail hour came early,
  Yet he was devoid of thirst
  For the blood of the accurst,
  Inconsiderate Tagallo
  (Seas of gore, however shallow,

He regarded very lightly,
As inutile and unsightly);
So he did not much frequent
That insurrectionary gent.

Captain Purvis went a-scouting
(Truth to tell, he took an outing)—
Found a Filipino sleeping,
Bound and took him into keeping.
Calling Sergeant-Major Gump,
They conveyed him to a pump,
Laid him on his back beneath,
With his tongue between his teeth.
Said the captain: "We'll not thump him,
But he is a spy—we'll pump him.
That's our duty; information,
Secrets useful to the nation,
We'll wring from him. Tell me, sir,
Tell me truly, why a cur
Wags its tail—and, furthermore,
When a door is not a door."

But that person obstinacious
Answered, with a look ungracious,
That he'd see them (he was witty)
Both in Helfurst—that's a city

In Silesia, I suppose,
Where no proper person goes.
So they pumped him full of water—
Son of Temperance, or Daughter,
Ne'er was half so full as that,
Nor any poison-fevered rat
Trying with a fervor frantic
To abolish the Atlantic.
Yes, that Filipino bloated
Till his snowy liver floated
Like a lily on a pond.
And his soul to the Beyond
Drifted on the strong, full tide,
"By word of mouth," from his inside.

Captain Purvis being duly
Tried, the President said: "Truly,
He's a water-warrior; he
Would more fitly serve at sea."
So the Navy broke his fall—
Rearest-Admiral of all!
By his ironclad desk he's sitting,
Sometimes writing, sometimes knitting,
For he's Chief (and that's enough)
Of the Bureau of Plum Duff.

1902.

ANOTHER ASPIRANT

George Dewey, dear, I did not think that you—
So very married and so happy, too—
Would go philandering with another girl
And give your gay mustache a fetching curl
And set your cap—I should say your cocked hat—
At Miss Columbia the like o' that.
Pray what can you expect to get by throwing
Sheep's eyes at one so very, very knowing?

See how she served McKinley! All his life
He wooed her for his morganatic wife,
Swore that he loved her better than his soul
(I'm half inclined to think, upon the whole,
She better did deserve his love) then vowed
He'd marry her alive, or even aloud!
What did she? Ere his breath he could recover
She heartlessly accepted that poor lover!

There's William Bryan of the silver tongue,
Old in ambition, in discretion young—
He courts her with the song, the dance, the lute,
But knows how suitors feel who do not suit.
And Teddy Roosevelt, plucking from its sheath
The weapon that he wears behind his teeth,

Endeavors in his simple, soldier fashion,
But all in vain, to touch her heart by slashin'.

Beware, my web-foot friend, beware her wiles:
Fly from her sighs and disregard her smiles.
She's no fool mermaid with a comb and glass,
But Satan's daughter with a breast of brass.
Put out your prow to sea again—but hold!
If Bryan and McKinley, all too bold,
Show up along the beach with little Teddy—
Well, Dewey, you may fire when you are ready.

    April, 1900.

A LEARNER

I do not think you rightly understand:
  My foolish tongue imperfectly has caught
  The trick of loving words, nor, as it ought,
Serves the sweet purpose of the heart's command.
Dear, I'm untraveled in the golden land
  Of love, and in its language all untaught,
  Like some poor mariner by tempest brought
'Mongst alien races to a foreign strand.
So, pretty native, bear with me until
  My simple wants I rightly can avow—

My will to serve you with my men and ships.
For lo! already I've some little skill
In the strange tongue.   Ask me to kiss you now—
I'll read the riddle ere it leaves your lips!

TO BRIDGET

Have ye heard what the news is, me darlint?
  The Fenians have threatened the Pope!
But, begorra, I think there's a snarl in't
  That's twisted it up like a rope,
  From a kink in the telescope.
For the news, ye must know, Biddy, reaches
  This counthry by means of a wire;
And sometimes the heat o' the speeches
  Just warrups it up like a fire.
Faith! who but the Divil would bother
The likes o' the Howly Father?

And the Divil is in it, I'm fearin',
  When a gintleman's called on to chuse
Betwixt Howly Church and Ould Erin—
  The shamrock and harp to refuse,
  Or be like the murtherin' Jews.
Och! Biddy, me mind it is troublin'
  To know where me body's at home—

With half o' me sowl there in Dublin
  And t'other half over in Rome!
Bedad, there's a shplit in the party
Of the name of O'Malley McCarty!

AFTER TENNYSON

You ask me why, though ill at ease,
  Within this region I subsist,
  Where honor's dead, and law is hissed,
And all men pillage as they please.

It is the land where freemen kill
  In warm debate their party foes;
  The land where judges come to blows
And speak the things that make us ill;

A land of base expedient;
  A land where gold can justice drown;
  Where Freedom's chains are handed down
From President to President;

Where factions wrangle for the bread
  Of honest men; where, fearing naught,

Accurst monopolies have caught
The people in the nets they spread;

Where branded convicts execute
    The laws that in a better time
    They broke, and every kind of crime
Stalks unashamed and resolute.

Should honor e'er possess the land,
    And patriots control the State,
    And Justice rise, divine with hate,
To choke the politician band,

O waft me from the harbor forth,
    Wild winds. I'll see Alaska's sky.
    Here 'twill have grown too warm, and I
Will run for office in the North.

TO MY BIRD

If I were screaming in a cage,
    Parrot mine, parrot mine,
And you were rhyming on this page,
    Parrot mine,

I'd try to shriek a fresher bit
Of wisdom to excite your wit,
    Parrot mine.

All you have said is nothing new,
    Parrot mine, parrot mine,
By Jove, I taught it all to you,
    Parrot mine.
While you nor can, nor could, nor might
Have thought what I could care to write,
    Parrot mine.

Your life in order to maintain,
    Parrot mine, parrot mine,
You daily dine upon my brain,
    Parrot mine.
My mind, a torn and mangled wreck,
Is disappearing down your neck,
    Parrot mine.

Well, be it so: present your bill,
    Parrot mine, parrot mine,
And on my virtues feast your fill,
    Parrot mine.
My vices, though, will disagree
With you, my pet. They do with me,
    Parrot mine.

BUSINESS

Two villains of the highest rank
Set out one night to rob a bank.
They found the building, looked it o'er,
Each window noted, tried each door,
Scanned carefully the lidded hole
For minstrels to cascade the coal—
In short, examined five-and-twenty
Short cuts from poverty to plenty.
But all were sealed, they saw full soon,
Against the minions of the moon.
" Enough," said one: " I'm satisfied."
The other, smiling fair and wide,
 Said: " I'm as highly pleased as you:
No burglar ever can get through.
Fate surely prospers our design—
The booty all is yours and mine."
So, full of hope, the following day
To the exchange they took their way
And bought, with manner free and frank,
Some stock of that devoted bank;
And they became, inside the year,
One President and one Cashier.

Their crime I can no further trace—
The means of safety to embrace,
I overdrew and left the place.

A POSSIBILITY

If the wicked gods were willing
  (Pray it never may be true!)
That a universal chilling
    Should ensue
Of the sentiment of loving,—
  If they made a great undoing
Of the plan of turtle-doving,
  Then farewell all poet-lore,
    Evermore.
If there were no more of billing
  There would be no more of cooing
And we all should be but owls—
    Lonely fowls
Blinking wonderfully wise,
  With our great round eyes—
Sitting singly in the gloaming and no longer two
  and two,
As unwilling to be wedded as unpracticed how
  to woo;

With regard to being mated,
Asking still with aggravated
Ungrammatical acerbity: " To who? To who? "

TO A CENSOR

The delay granted by the weakness and good nature of our
judges is responsible for half the murders.—*Daily Newspaper.*

Delay responsible? Why, then, my friend,
Impeach Delay and you will make an end.
Thrust vile Delay in jail and let it rot
For doing all the things that it should not.
Put not good-natured judges under bond,
But make Delay in damages respond.
Minos, Æacus, Rhadamanthus, rolled
Into one pitiless, unsmiling scold—
Unsparing censor, be your thongs uncurled
To " lash the rascals naked through the world."
The rascals? Nay, Rascality's the thing
Above whose back your knotted scourges sing.
Your satire, truly, like a razor keen,
" Wounds with a touch that's neither felt nor seen; "
For naught that you assail with falchion free
Has either nerves to feel or eyes to see.
Against abstractions evermore you charge:
You hack no helmet and you need no targe.

That wickedness is wrong and sin a vice,
That wrong's not right, nor foulness ever nice,
Fearless affirm.   All consequences dare:
Smite the offense and the offender spare.
When Ananias and Sapphira lied
Falsehood, had you been there, had surely died.
When money-changers in the Temple sat,
At money-changing you'd have whirled the "cat"
(That John-the-Baptist of the modern pen)
And all those brokers would have cried amen!

Good friend, if any judge deserve your blame
Have you no courage, or has he no name?
Upon his method will you wreak your wrath,
Himself all unmolested in his path?
Fall to! fall to!—your club no longer draw
To beat the air or flail a man of straw.
Scorn to do justice like the Saxon thrall
Who cuffed the offender's shadow on a wall.
Let rascals in the flesh attest your zeal—
Knocked on the mazzard or tripped up at heel!

We know that judges are corrupt.   We know
That crimes are lively and that laws are slow.
We know that lawyers lie and doctors slay;
That priests and preachers are but birds of pray;

That merchants cheat and journalists for gold
Flatter the vicious while at vice they scold.
'Tis all familiar as the simple lore
That two policemen and two thieves make four.

But since, while some are wicked some are good,
(As trees may differ though they all are wood)
Names here and there, to show whose head is hit,
The bad would sentence and the good acquit.
In sparing everybody none you spare:
Rebukes most personal are least unfair.
To fire at random if you still prefer,
And swear at Dog but never kick a cur,
Permit me yet one ultimate appeal
To something that you understand and feel:
Let thrift and vanity your heart persuade—
You might be read if you would learn your trade.

Good brother censors (you have doubtless guessed
Not one of you but all are here addressed)
Remember this: the shaft that seeks a heart
Draws all eyes after it; an idle dart
Shot at some shadow flutters o'er the green,
Its flight unheeded and its fall unseen.

"THE WHOLE WORLD KIN"

" Liars for witnesses; for lawyers brutes
Willing to lose their souls to win their suits;
Cowards for jurors, and for judge a clown
Who ne'er took up the law, yet lays it down;
Justice denied, authority abused,
And the one blameless person the accused—
Thy courts, my country, all these dreadful years,
Move fools to laughter and the wise to tears."

So moaned an alien from beyond the foam.
Come here, my lad, I think you'll feel at home.

A FUTURE CONVERSATION

If the coal strike is not settled satisfactorily I shall lead
the wives of the miners in a march on Washington.—*Mother
Jones.*

" What is this I see, what is this I see
In this year of our Lord 3003?
What ruins are spread in confusion wide
Over hill and plain by Potomac's side? "

" These, traveler, these are the leveled stones
Attesting the prowess of Mother Jones."

"O plowman, I never in history grew
To the high attainments of Smith Carew,
Whose noble book, 'The Decline and Fall
Of America,' holds the respect of all.
Of Mother Jones I often have heard,
But thought—pray pardon if I have erred—
That the ancient lady became renowned
By embroidering cats on a velvet ground."

"Your error is wide, remote, extreme:
Not the needle's shine, but the sabre's gleam
Delighted of old her heroic soul
And made her unloved of the Lords of Coal.
In that distant day when the miner 'rose,'
And to spite his countenance severed his nose,
And owners permitted each mine of the trust
To fill up with water to lay his dust,
She marshaled the women, with sabre and gun,
And marched with banners on Washington."

"I see, I see in these ruins gray
Through which you are urging your plowshare gay
The work of their hands, slender and white,
That plied the pick and the crowbar bright."

"The cannon, my friend,—but no harm was done,
For before the city was overrun

By the warrior-dames of that rebel rout
The politicians had cleaned it out,
And the stones that about the plain they spread
Were served to the poor when they asked for bread."

"O affable plowman, I'd fain admire
Your tale, but, alas, I'm myself a liar!
Besides, I've a better one, which, mayhap,
You'd like to be hearing."

                                        "Giddap, giddap!"

THE HESITATING VETERAN

When I was young and full of faith
    And other fads that youngsters cherish
A cry rose as of one that saith
    With emphasis: "Help or I perish!"
'Twas heard in all the land, and men
    The sound were each to each repeating.
It made my heart beat faster then
    Than any heart can now be beating.

For the world is old and the world is gray—
    Grown prudent and, I think, more witty.
She's cut her wisdom teeth, they say,
    And doesn't now go in for Pity.

Besides, the melancholy cry
  Was that of one, 'tis now conceded,
Whose plight no one beneath the sky
  Felt half so poignantly as he did.

Moreover, he was black. And yet
  That sentimental generation
With an austere compassion set
  Its face and faith to the occasion.
Then there were hate and strife to spare,
  And various hard knocks a-plenty;
And I ('twas more than my true share,
  I must confess) took five-and-twenty.

That all is over now—the reign
  Of love and trade stills all dissensions,
And the clear heavens arch again
  Above a land of peace and pensions.
The black chap—at the last we gave
  Him everything that he had cried for,
Though many white chaps in the grave
  'Twould puzzle to say what they died for.

I hope he's better off—I trust
  That his society and his master's
Are worth the price we paid, and must
Continue paying, in disasters;

But sometimes doubts press thronging round
   ('Tis mostly when my hurts are aching)
If war for Union was a sound
   And profitable undertaking.

'Tis said they mean to take away
   The Negro's vote for he's unlettered.
'Tis true he sits in darkness day
   And night, as formerly, when fettered;
But pray observe—howe'er he vote
   To whatsoever party turning,
He'll be with gentlemen of note
   And wealth and consequence and learning.

With saints and sages on each side,
   How could a fool through lack of knowledge,
Vote wrong? If learning is no guide
   Why ought one to have been in college?
O Son of Day, O Son of Night!
   What are your preferences made of?
I know not which of you is right,
   Nor which to be the more afraid of.

The world is old and the world is bad,
   And creaks and grinds upon its axis;
And man's an ape and the gods are mad!—
   There's nothing sure, not even our taxes.

No mortal man can Truth restore,
  Or say where she is to be sought for.
I know what uniform I wore—
  O, that I knew which side I fought for!

A YEAR'S " CASUALTIES "

Slain as they lay by the secret, slow,
Pitiless hand of an unseen foe,
Two score thousand old soldiers have crossed
The river to join the loved and lost.
In the space of a year their spirits fled,
Silent and white, to the camp of the dead.

One after one they fall asleep
And the pension agents awake to weep,
And orphaned statesmen are loud in their wail
As the souls flit by on the evening gale.
O Father of Battles, pray give us release
From the horrors of peace, the horrors of peace!

TO-DAY

I saw a man who knelt in prayer,
  And heard him say:
" I'll lay my inmost spirit bare
  To-day.

" Lord, for to-morrow and its need
　　I do not pray;
Let me upon my neighbor feed
　　To-day.

" Let me my duty duly shirk
　　And run away
From any form or phase of work
　　To-day.

" From Thy commands exempted still,
　　Let me obey
The promptings of my private will
　　To-day.

" Let me no word profane, no lie,
　　Unthinking, say
If any one is standing by
　　To-day.

" My secret sins and vices grave
　　Let none betray;
The scoffer's jeers I do not crave
　　To-day.

" And if to-day my fortune all
　　Should ebb away

Help me on other men's to fall
    To-day.

"So, for to-morrow and its mite
  I do not pray;
Just give me everything in sight
    To-day."

I cried: "Amen!" He rose and ran
  Like oil away.
I said: "I've seen an honest man
    To-day."

AN ALIBI

A famous journalist who long
Had told the great unheaded throng
Whate'er they thought, by day or night,
Was true as Holy Writ, and right,
Was caught in—well, on second thought,
It is enough that he was caught
And, thrown into a jail, became
The fuel of a public flame.
"*Vox populi vox Dei*," said
The jailer. Inxling bent his head

Without remark: that motto good
In bold-faced type had always stood
Above the columns where his pen
Had rioted in praise of men
And all they said—provided he
Was sure they mostly did agree.
Meanwhile a sharp and bitter strife
To take, or save, the culprit's life
Or liberty (which, I suppose,
Was much the same to him) arose
Outside. The journal that his pen
Adorned denounced his crime—but then
Its editor in secret tried
To have the indictment set aside.
The opposition papers swore
His father was a rogue before,
And all his wife's relations were
Like him and similar to her.
They begged their readers to subscribe
A dollar each to make a bribe
That any Judge would feel was large
Enough to prove the gravest charge—
Unless, it might be, the Defense
Put up superior evidence.
The law's traditional delay
Was all too short: the trial day
Dawned red and menacing. The Judge
Sat on the Bench and wouldn't budge,

And all the motions counsel made
Could not move *him*—and there he stayed.
"The case must now proceed," he said,
"While I am just, in heart and head.
It happens—as, indeed, it ought—
Both sides with equal sums have bought
My favor: I can try the cause
Impartially." (Prolonged applause.)

The prisoner was now arraigned
And said that he was greatly pained
To be suspected—*he,* whose pen
Had charged so many other men
With crimes and misdemeanors! "Why,"
He said, a tear in either eye,
"If men who live by crying out
'Stop thief!' are not themselves from doubt
Of their integrity exempt
Let all forego the vain attempt
To make a reputation! Sir,
I'm innocent, and I demur."
Whereat a thousand voices cried
That he indubitably lied—
Vox populi as loudly roared
As bull by *picadores* gored,
In his own coin receiving pay
To make a Spanish holiday.

The jury—twelve good men and true—
Were then sworn in to see it through,
And each made solemn oath that he
As any babe unborn was free
From prejudice, opinion, thought,
Respectability, brains—aught
That could disqualify; and some
Explained that they were deaf and dumb.
A better twelve, his Honor said,
Was rare, except among the dead.
The witnesses were called and sworn.
The tales they told made angels mourn,
And the Good Book they'd kissed became
Red with the consciousness of shame.
Whenever one of them approached
The truth, " That witness wasn't coached,
Your Honor!" cried the lawyers both.
"Strike out his testimony," quoth
The learned Judge; "this court denies
Its ear to stories that surprise.
I hold that witnesses exempt
From coaching all are in contempt."
Both Prosecution and Defense
Applauded the judicial sense,
And the spectators all averred
Such wisdom they had never heard:
'Twas plain the prisoner would be
Found guilty in the first degree.

Meanwhile that wight's pale cheek confessed
The nameless terrors in his breast.
He felt remorseful, too, because
He wasn't half they said he was.
" If I'd been such a rogue," he mused
On opportunities unused,
" I might have easily become
As wealthy as Methusalum."
This journalist adorned, alas,
The middle, not the Bible, class.

With equal skill the lawyers' pleas
Attested their divided fees.
Each gave the other one the lie,
Then helped him frame a sharp reply.
Good Lord! it was a bitter fight,
And lasted all the day and night.
When once or oftener the roar
Had silenced the judicial snore
The speaker suffered for the sport
By fining for contempt of court.
Twelve jurors' noses good and true
Unceasing sang the trial through,
And even *vox populi* was spent
In rattles through a nasal vent.
Clerk, bailiff, constables and all
Heard Morpheus sound the trumpet call

To arms—his arms—and all fell in
Save counsel for the Man of Sin.
That thaumaturgist stood and swayed
The wand their faculties obeyed—
That magic wand, which, like a flame,
Leaped, wavered, quivered and became
A wonder-worker—known among
The ignoble vulgar as a Tongue.

How long, O Lord, how long my verse
Runs on for better or for worse
In meter which o'ermasters me,
Octosyllabically free!—
A meter, which, the poets say,
No power of restraint can stay;—
A hard-mouthed meter, suited well
To him who, having naught to tell,
Must hold attention as a trout
Is held by paying out and out
The slender line which else would break
Should one attempt the fish to take.
Thus tavern guides who've naught to show
But some adjacent curio
By devious trails their patrons lead
And make them think 'tis far indeed.
Where was I?
                    While the lawyer talked
The rogue took up his feet and walked:

While all about him loudly slept,
Into the street he calmly stepped.
In very truth, the man who thought
The people's voice from heaven had caught
God's inspiration took a change
Of venue—it was passing strange!
Straight to his editor he went
And that ingenious person sent
A Negro to impersonate
The fugitive.   In adequate
Disguise he took the vacant place
And buried in his arms his face.
When all was done the lawyer stopped
And silence like a bombshell dropped
Upon the court: Judge, jury, all
Within that venerable hall
(Except the deaf and dumb, indeed,
And one or two whom death had freed)
Awoke and tried to look as though
Slumber was all they did not know.

And now that tireless lawyer-man
Took breath, and then again began:
"Your Honor, if you did attend
To what I've urged (my learned friend
Nodded concurrence) to support
The motion I have made, this court

May soon adjourn. With your assent
I've shown abundant precedent
For introducing now, though late,
New evidence to exculpate
My client. So, if you'll allow,
I'll prove an *alibi!*"   "What?—how?"
Stammered the Judge. "Well, yes, I can't
Deny your showing, and I grant
The motion. Do I understand
You undertake to prove—good land!—
That when the crime—you mean to show
Your client wasn't *there?* "   " O, no,
I cannot quite do that, I find:
My *alibi's* another kind
Of *alibi*—I'll make it clear,
Your Honor, that he isn't *here.*"
The Darky here upreared his head,
Tranquillity affrighted fled
And consternation reigned instead!

A MEETING

"Good morning," said Garfield, extending his hand,
To Mr. Parnell in the Heavenly Land.
"Good morning, good morning," said Mr. Parnell;
" I hope (though 'tis needless to ask) you are well.

How sweetly that chorus of cherubim sings!
Pray how do you manage these cumbersome wings?
This halo—I dare say I'm terribly green,
But somehow I can't make it hold my dudheen.
This harp is all right, but the shamrock I miss,
And—O, by the way, in this region of bliss
I trust that the rascally schemer who wrote
The Morey epistle, which lost you the vote
Electoral, I am not likely to meet?"

Then Garfield, his eyes on the cloud at his feet,
Burned in the cheeks with a fervor divine
That conquered his halo's inferior shine;
Then said, with a look that was level and far:
"I fear (to be honest and frank) that you are.
The person who wrote that mysterious, queer,
Bad letter is here—ah, exceedingly here."
And he smiled in an infantile sort of a way,
Like a man with a qualm, and went on to say:
"I'm happy to meet you. What news from below?
Did it look when you left there as if they would show
Who wrote, with a villainous purpose in view,
The peppery letters imputed to you?"

Said Mr. Parnell: "Yes, it did, I must say—
In fact, that's the reason I hastened away."

'Then they sang a psalm, and they sang so well
That Murchison heard it while sobbing in Hell.

J. F. B.

How well this man unfolded to our view
    The world's beliefs of Death and Heaven and
        Hell—
    This man whose own convictions none could tell,
Nor if his maze of reason had a clew.
Dogmas he wrote for daily bread, but knew
    The fair philosophies of doubt so well
    That while we listened to his words there fell
Some that were strangely comforting if true.
Marking how wise we grew upon his doubt,
    We said: "If so, by groping in the night,
    He can proclaim some certain paths of trust,
How great our profit if he saw about
    His feet the highways leading to the light."
    Now he sees all. Ah, Christ! his mouth is dust!

THE DYING STATESMAN

    It is a politician man—
        He draweth near his end,
    And friends weep round that partisan,
        Of every man the friend.

Between the Known and the Unknown
  He lieth on the strand;
The light upon the sea is thrown
  That lay upon the land.

It shineth in his glazing eye,
  It burneth on his face;
God send that when we come to die
  We know that sign of grace!

Upon his lips his blessed sprite
  Poiseth her joyous wing.
" How is it with thee, child of light?
  Dost hear the angels sing? "

" The song I hear, the crown I see,
  And know that God is love.
Farewell, dark world—I go to be
  A postmaster above! "

For him no monumental arch,
  But, O, 'tis good and brave
To see the Grand Old Party march
  To office o'er his grave!

THE DEATH OF GRANT

Father! whose hard and cruel law
  Is part of thy compassion's plan,
  Thy works presumptuously we scan
For what the prophets say they saw.

Unbidden still the awful slope
  Walling us in we climb to gain
  Assurance of the shining plain
That faith has certified to hope.

In vain!—beyond the circling hill
  The shadow and the cloud abide.
  Subdue the doubt, our spirits guide
To trust the record and be still.

To trust it loyally as he
  Who, heedful of his high design,
  Ne'er raised a seeking eye to thine,
But wrought thy will unconsciously,

Disputing not of chance or fate,
  Nor questioning of cause or creed;
  For anything but duty's deed
Too simply wise, too humbly great.

The cannon syllabled his name;
  His shadow shifted o'er the land,
  Portentous, as at his demand
Successive bastions sprang to flame!

He flared the continent with fire,
  The rivers ran in lines of light!
  Thy will be done on earth—if right
Or wrong he cared not to inquire.

His was the heavy hand, and his
  The service of the despot blade;
  His the soft answer that allayed
War's giant animosities.

Let us have peace: our clouded eyes,
  Fill, Father, with another light,
  That we may see with clearer sight
Thy servant's soul in Paradise.

THE FOUNTAIN REFILLED

Of Hans Pietro Shanahan
(Who was a most ingenious man)
The Muse of History records
That he'd get drunk as twenty lords.

He'd get so truly drunk that men
Stood by to marvel at him when
His slow advance along the street
Was but a vain cycloidal feat.

And when 'twas fated that he fall
With a wide, geographic sprawl,
They signified assent by sounds
Heard (faintly) at its utmost bounds.

And yet this Mr. Shanahan
(Who was a most ingenious man)
Cast not on wine his thirsty eyes
When it was red or otherwise.

All malt or spirituous tope
He loathed as cats dissent from soap;
And cider, if it touched his lip,
Evoked a groan at every sip.

But still, as heretofore explained,
He not infrequently was grained.
(I'm not of those who call it "corned"—
Coarse speech I've always duly scorned.)

Though, truth to say, and that's but right,
Strong drink (it hath an adder's bite!)

Was what had put him in the mud,
The only kind he used was blood!

Alas that an immortal soul
Addicted to the flowing bowl
The emptied flagon should again
Replenish from a neighbor's vein!

But, Mr. Shanahan was so
Constructed, and his taste that low.
Not more deplorable was he
In kind of thirst than in degree;

For sometimes fifty souls would pay
The debt of nature in a day
To free him from the shame and pain
Of dread Sobriety's misreign.

His native land, with a proud sense
Of his unique inabstinence,
Abated something of its pride
At thought of his unfilled inside;

And some the boldness had to say
'Twere well if he were called away
To slake his thirst for evermore
In oceans of celestial gore.

But Hans Pietro Shanahan
(Who was a most ingenious man)
Knew that his thirst was mortal; so
Remained unsainted here below—

Unsainted and unsaintly, for
He neither went to glory nor
To abdicate his power deigned
Where, under Providence, he reigned,

But kept his Boss's power accurst
To serve his wild uncommon thirst,
Which now had grown so truly great
It was a drain upon the State.

Soon, soon there came a time, alas!
When he turned down an empty glass—
All practicable means were vain
His special wassail to obtain.

In vain poor Decimation tried
To furnish forth the needful tide;
And Civil War as vainly shed
Its niggard offering of red.

Poor Shanahan! his thirst increased
Until he wished himself deceased,

Invoked the firearm and the knife,
But could not die to save his life!

He was so dry his own veins made
No answer to the seeking blade;
  So weak that when he would have passed
Away he could not breathe his last.

'Twas then, when almost in despair,
(Unlaced his shoon, unkempt his hair)
He saw as in a dream a way
To wet afresh his mortal clay.

Yes, Hans Pietro Shanahan
(Who was a most ingenious man)
Saw freedom, and with joy and pride
"Thalassa! (or Thalatta!)" cried.

Straight to the alderman went he,
With many a " pull " and many a fee,
And many a most corrupt " combine "
(The Press for twenty cents a line

Held out and fought him—O God bless
Forevermore the holy Press!)

Till he had franchises complete
For trolley lines on every street!

The cars were builded and, they say,
Were run on rails laid every way—
Rhomboidal roads, and circular,
And oval—everywhere a car—

Square, dodecagonal (in great
Esteem the form called Figure 8)
And many other kinds of form
As different as paths of storm.

No other group of men's abodes
E'er had so odd electric roads,
Which, winding in and winding out,
Began and ended all about.

No city had, unless in Mars,
That city's fatal gift of cars.
They ran by day, they flew by night,
And O, the sorry, sorry sight!

And Hans Pietro Shanahan
(Who was a most ingenious man)
Incessantly, the Muse records,
Lay drunk as twenty thousand lords!

LAUS LUCIS

Theosophists are about to build a "Temple for the Revival
of the Mysteries of Antiquity."—*Vide the Newspapers, passim.*

Each to his taste: some men prefer to play
At mystery, and others at piquet.
Some sit in mystic meditation; some
Parade the street with tambourine and drum.
One studies to decipher ancient lore
Which, proving stuff, he studies all the more;
Another swears that learning is but good
To darken things already understood,
Then writes upon Simplicity so well
That none agree on what he wants to tell,
And future ages will declare his pen
Inspired by gods with messages to men.
To found an ancient order, these devote
Their time—with ritual, regalia, goat,
Blankets for tossing, chairs of little ease
And all the modern inconveniences;
Those, saner, frown upon unmeaning rites
And go to church for rational delights.
So all are suited, shallow and profound,
The prophets prosper and the world goes round.
For me—unread in the occult, I'm fain
To damn all mysteries alike as vain,

Spurn the obscure and base my faith upon
The Revelations of the good St. John.

NANINE

We heard a song-bird trilling—
  'Twas but a day ago.
Such rapture he was rilling
  As only we could know.

This morning he is flinging
  His music from the tree,
But something in the singing
  Is not the same to me.

His inspiration fails him,
  Or he has lost his skill.
Nanine, Nanine, what ails him
  That he should sing so ill?

Nanine is not replying—
  She hears no earthly song.
The sun and bird are lying
  And the night is, O, so long!

TECHNOLOGY

'Twas a serious person with locks of gray
   And a figure like a crescent;
His gravity, clearly, had come to stay,
   But his smile was evanescent.

He stood and conversed with a neighbor and
   With (likewise) a high falsetto;
And he stabbed his forefinger into his hand
   As if it had been a stiletto.

His words, like the notes of a tenor drum,
   Came out of his head unblended,
And the wonderful altitude of some
   Was exceptionally splendid.

While executing a shake of the head,
   With the hand, as it were, of a master,
This agonizing old gentleman said:
   " 'Twas a truly sad disaster!

" Four hundred and ten longs and shorts in all,
   Went down "—he paused and snuffled.

A single tear was observed to fall,
   And the old man's drum was muffled.

"A very calamitous year," he said,
   And again his head-piece hoary
He shook, and another pearl he shed,
   As if he wept *con amore*.

"O lacrymose person," I cried, "pray why
   Should these failures so affect you?
With speculators in stocks no eye
   That's normal would ever connect you."

He focused his orbs upon mine and smiled
   In a sinister sort of manner.
"Young man," he said, "your words are wild:
   I spoke of the steamship 'Hanner.'

"For she has went down in a howlin' squall,
   And my heart is nigh to breakin'—
Four hundred and ten longs and shorts in all
   Will never need undertakin'!

"I'm in the business myself," said he,
   "And you've mistook my expression;
For I uses the technical terms, you see,
   Employed in my perfession."

That old undertaker has joined the throng
　On the other side of the River,
But I'm still unhappy to think I'm a " long,"
　And a tape-line makes me shiver.

A REPLY TO A LETTER

O nonsense, parson—tell me not they thrive
　And jubilate who follow your dictation.
The good are the unhappiest lot alive—
　I know they are from careful observation.
　If freedom from the terrors of damnation
Lengthens the visage like a telescope,
And lacrymosity's a sign of hope,
　Then I'll continue, in my dreadful plight,
To tread the dusky paths of sin, and grope
　Contentedly without your lantern's light;
　And though in many a bog beslubbered quite,
Refuse to flay me with ecclesiastic soap.

You say 'tis a sad world, seeing I'm condemned,
　With many a million others of my kidney.
Each continent's Hammed, Japheted and Shemmed
　With sinners—worldlings like Sir Philip Sidney
And scoffers like Voltaire, who thought it bliss
To simulate respect for Genesis—

Who bent the mental knee as if in prayer,
But mocked at Moses underneath his hair,
And like an angry gander bowed his head to hiss.

Seeing such as these, who die without contrition,
Must go to—beg your pardon, sir—perdition,
  The sons of light, you tell me, can't be gay,
But count it sin of the sort called omission
  The groan to smother or the tear to stay
  Or fail to—what is that they live by?—pray.
So down they kneel, and the whole serious race is
Put by divine compassion on a praying basis.

Well, if you take it so to heart, while yet
  Our own hearts are so light with nature's leaven,
You'll weep indeed when we in Hades sweat,
  And you look down upon us out of Heaven.
In fancy, lo! I see your wailing shades
Thronging the crystal battlements. Cascades
Of tears spring singing from each golden spout,
  Run roaring from the verge with hoarser sound,
  Dash downward through the glimmering pro-
        found,
Quench the tormenting flame and put the Devil out!

Presumptuous fool! to you no power belongs
To pitchfork me to Heaven upon the prongs

Of a bad pen, whose disobedient sputter,
With less of ink than incoherence fraught,
    Befits the folly that it tries to utter.
    Brains, I observe, as well as tongues, can stutter:
You suffer from impediment of thought,
    Save when considering your bread-and-butter.

When next you " point the way to Heaven," take care:
Your fingers being thumbs, point Heaven knows
        where!
Farewell, poor dunce! your letter though I blame,
Bear witness how my anger I can tame:
I've called you everything except your hateful name!

TO OSCAR WILDE

Because from Folly's lips you got
    Some babbled mandate to subdue
    The realm of Common Sense, and you
Made promise and considered not,—

Because you strike a random blow
    At what you do not understand,
    And beckon with a friendly hand
To something that you do not know,

I hold no speech of your desert,
   Nor baffle with porrected shield
   The wooden weapon that you wield,
But meet you with a cast of dirt.

Dispute with such a thing as you—
   Twin show to the two-headed calf?
   Why, sir, if I repress my laugh,
'Tis more than half the world can do.
   1882.

BORN LEADERS OF MEN

Tuckerton Tamerlane Morey Mahosh
   Is a statesman of world-wide fame,
With a notable knack at rhetorical bosh
   To glorify somebody's name—
Somebody chosen by Tuckerton's masters
To succor the country from divers disasters
   Portentous to Mr. Mahosh.

Percy O'Halloran Tarpy Cabee
   Is in the political swim.
He cares not a button for men, not he:
   Great principles captivate him—

Principles cleverly cut out and fitted
To Percy's capacity, duly admitted
    And fought for by Mr. Cabee.

    Drusus Tum Swinnerton Porfer Fitzurse
      Holds office the most of his life.
    For men nor for principles cares he a curse
      But much for his neighbor's wife.
The Ship of State leaks, but *he* doesn't pump any—
Messrs. Mahosh, Cabee & Company
    Pump for good Mr. Fitzurse.

THE CRIME OF 1903

Time was, not very long ago,
    As by historians time is reckoned,
When first of virtues here below
Was hatred of secession, though
    Some swore it wasn't even second;
But these (they mostly were down South)
    Have all renounced their view with candor—
Some tardily by word of mouth,
    Some, earlier, in a manner grander.

To stamp their error out, 'tis true,
    We paid enough of blood (the treasure

Would pave with gold an avenue)
To float a battleship or two,
   If so the cost we choose to measure.
'Twas worth it all, we say and say—
   The President has often said it;
And so it was—to *us;* and they
   Say nothing, as a rule, who shed it.

" Times change and we change with them,"
     men
   Of old renown averred in Latin;
And that's as true on tongue or pen
This blessed century as when
   The seat of empire Cæsar sat in.
For see how many play their parts
   As ardent lovers of secession,
Promoting it with all their hearts—
   In countries out of our possession.

O men of variable views,
   How can you be so light and fickle?
Is it because you think the news
From Panama portends no bruise
   To you, nor payment of a nickel?
Nay, is it that you scent a gain
   In troubles of a neighbor nation,
And so appraise her loss and pain
   As nothing worth a valuation?

Those ills 'tis easy to endure
    That light upon and sting another—
That's Christian fortitude; but sure
There's somewhere an account of your
    Least feeling toward a hapless brother.
Himself may show by deed and speech
    Less racial sympathies than tribal,
But—well, this is no place to preach;
    The sermon's mostly in the Bible.

We're false to trust and quick to spy
    The fissure in a friendly armor,
Even Freedom can no more rely
    Upon our promise not to harm her.
O Guardian of Continents,
    My country! shall that evil dower,
The passion for preëminence,
Cry from thy seaward battlements
    A soul already drunk with power?
    1903.

FOR EXPULSION

They say, Brig. Roberts, you have seven wives,
    And every one a beauty! As to that
I'm not informed; in the domestic hives
    Of Utah, where I've sometimes hung my hat,

Not all the dames were comely. Like a cat
That has nine lives and must support them all,
  You have to hustle round a bit, I fancy.
Now don't you really agree with Paul
  That women are the devil?—even Nancy
And Mary Jane and Caroline and Ella
And Ruth and Adeline and Isabella!

If I had half as many wives as you
  (That's three wives and a half as I compute)
I hardly know what I'd be driven to.
  I might in desperation play the flute,
  Or Congress find in me a raw recruit.
Then, I suppose, the country would uprise
  And say the things I least should care to hear:
And virtuous editors would damn my eyes,
  And cartilaginous virgins pain my ear,
And now and then some pious person clamor,
Blessed with one wife, ten wenches and no grammar.

All that and more you're suffering, my friend,
  For, having married all the maids you saw,
You contumaciously refuse to bend
  A corrigible back to altered law
  And leave them (all but one) lamenting. Pshaw!
Don't be so squeamish. Yes, the children may
  Lament a little too when made acquainted

With their mischance in being put away,
   And your own countenance with shame be painted;
But that's the smallest price for which we'll sell
A seat in Congress and a bed in Hell.

JUDEX JOCOSUS

We blench when maniacs to dance begin.
What makes a skull so dreadful is the grin.
When horrible and ludicrous unite,
Our sense of humor does but feed our fright.
As the shocked spirit with a double dread
Might see a monkey watching by the dead,
Or headsman part a neck, without a fault,
While turning o'er the block a somersault.
So, Judge Hilario, the untroubled awe
And reverence men cherish for the law
Turn all to terror when with wit profound
And tricksy humor *you* the law expound.
More frightful sounds the felon's doom by half
From lips still twisted to an idiot laugh.

"GRAFT"

Cuba, our pupil, let thy glory shine—
Our own is brighter, but effulgent thine!
Lately thine arms struck terror to the foe,
And now thy hands bring treasuries to woe!
Daughter of Terrors, Mother of Alarms,
Courage himself may fly before thine arms;
But O, what thing escapes, what thing withstands,
The power of those comprehensive hands?

THE TALE OF A CRIME

Once, in the olden time, a certain King
(But where he reigned I know not) said: "Go bring
My Chief Adviser here before the throne,
And cut his head off clear down to the bone!"
"With pleasure, Sire," said—keen to earn his wage—
The High Dissuader from the Sin of Age;
"But kings should still be civil, even when just:
You'll charge the villain with some crime, I trust?"

"Why, that's no more than fair," the King replied.
They brought the culprit in, securely tied,

And the King said: " Let some one who can read
Stand forward and unfold the Golden Screed,
Bright with the names of all the sins and crimes
And vices ever known from ancient times.
We'll fit the fellow for the headsman's prank
With one appropriate to his face and rank."

In drowsy monotone the Lector read
The shining list, beginning at the head.
(*Lèse majesté* was naturally first—
Of crimes conceivable, the blackest, worst!)
As each was named the prisoner addressed
The throne and, as the law compelled, confessed.
'Twas fatal not to: in that olden day
Little was heard about the law's delay.

But still the royal taste could find for him
No crime well suited to the royal whim,
And, wearied by the reader's droning voice,
The sovereign fell asleep, nor made a choice—
Snored like an organ till the stones were jarred
Distinguishing the palace from the yard.
Meantime, the accused continued to confess,
Each nod said " guilty " and each look said " yes."

And still the monarch slept: each courtier feared
To wake him lest himself should " lose his beard."

('Twas a fine euphemism, and meant his head—
Some things for prudence are obliquely said.)
" Finis," the reader said, and roundabout
Fell silence like a loud awakening shout!
The startled sovereign left a snore half-snored—
" That's what the scoundrel's guilty of!" he roared.

So there before the king upon his throne
They cut his head off clean down to the bone!
And all the devils made a joyous din
To celebrate the new and lovely sin.

TO THE BARTHOLDI STATUE

O Liberty, God-gifted—
    Young and immortal maid—
In your high hand uplifted,
    The torch declares your trade.

Its crimson menace, flaming
    Upon the sea and shore,
Is, trumpet-like, proclaiming
    That Law shall be no more.

Austere incendiary,
    We're blinking in the light;

Where is your customary
  Grenade of dynamite?

Where are your staves and switches
  For men of gentle birth?
Your mask and dirk for riches?
  Your chains for wit and worth?

Perhaps, you've brought the halters
  You used in the old days,
When round religion's altars
  You stabled Cromwell's bays?

Behind you, unsuspected,
  Have you the axe, fair wench,
Wherewith you once collected
  A poll-tax from the French?

America salutes you—
  Preparing to " disgorge."
Take everything that suits you,
  And marry Henry George.
  1894.

AN UNMERRY CHRISTMAS

Christmas, you tell me, comes but once a year.
One place it never comes, and that is here.
Here, in these pages no good wishes spring,
No well-worn greetings tediously ring—
For Christmas greetings are like pots of ore:
The hollower they are they ring the more.
Here shall no holly cast a spiny shade,
Nor mistletoe my solitude invade,
No trinket-laden vegetable come,
No jorum steam with Sheolate of rum.
No shrilling children shall their voices rear.
Hurrah for Christmas without Christmas cheer!

No presents, if you please—I know too well
What Herbert Spencer, if he didn't tell
(I know not if he did) yet might have told
Of present-giving in the days of old,
When Early Man with gifts propitiated
The chiefs whom most he doubted, feared and hated,
Or tendered them in hope to reap some rude
Advantage from the taker's gratitude.
Since thus the Gift its origin derives
(How much of its first character survives

You know as well as I) my stocking's tied,
My pocket buttoned—with my soul inside.
I save my money and I save my pride.

Dinner? Yes; thank you—just a baby's body
Done to a nutty brown, and a tear toddy
To give me appetite; and as to drink,
About a half a jug of blood, I think,
Will do; for still I love that good red wine,
Coagulating well, with wrinkles fine
Fretting the satin surface of its flood.
O tope of kings—divine Falernian—blood!

Duse take the shouting fowls upon the limb,
The kneeling cattle and the rising hymn!
Has not a pagan rights to be regarded—
His heart assaulted and his ear bombarded
With sentiments and sounds that good old Pan
Even in his demonium would ban?

No, friends—no Christmas here, for I have sworn
To keep my heart hard and my knees unworn.
Enough you have of jester, player, priest:
I as the skeleton attend your feast,
In the mad revelry to make a lull
With shaken finger and with bobbing skull.

However you my services may flout,
Philosophy disdain and reason doubt,
I mean to hold in customary state,
My dismal revelry and celebrate
My yearly rite until the crack o' doom,—
Ignore the cheerful season's warmth and bloom
And cultivate an oasis of gloom.

FROM VIRGINIA TO PARIS

The polecat, sovereign of its native wood,
Dashes damnation upon bad and good;
The health of all the upas trees impairs
By exhalations deadlier than theirs;
Poisons the rattlesnake and warts the toad—
The creeks go rotten and the rocks corrode!
She shakes o'er breathless hill and shrinking dale
The horrid aspergillus of her tail!
From every saturated hair, till dry,
The spargent fragrances divergent fly,
Stifle the world and reek along the sky!

Removed to alien scenes, amid the strife
Of urban odors to ungladden life—

Where gas and sewers and dead dogs conspire
The flesh to torture and the soul to fire—
Where all the "well defined and several stinks"
Known to mankind hold revel and high jinks—
Humbled in spirit, smitten with a sense
Of lost distinction, leveled eminence,
Her powers atrophied, her vigor sunk,
She lives deodorized, a sweeter skunk.

A "MUTE INGLORIOUS MILTON"

"O, I'm the Unaverage Man,
  But you never have heard of me,
For my brother, the Average Man, outran
  My fame with rapiditee,
  And I'm sunk in Oblivion's sea;
But my bully big brother the world can span
  With his wide notorietee.
I do everything that I can
  To make 'em attend to me,
But the papers ignore the Unaverage Man
  With a weird uniformitee."

So sang with a dolorous note
  A voice that I heard from the beach;

On the sable waters it seemed to float
  Like a mortal part of speech.
The sea was Oblivion's sea,
  And I cried as I plunged to swim:
" The Unaverage Man shall reside with me."
  But he didn't—I stayed with him!

THE FREE TRADER'S LAMENT

Oft from a trading-boat I purchased spice
  And shells and corals, brought for my inspection
From the fair tropics—paid a Christian price
And was content in my fool's paradise,
  Where never had been heard the word " Protection."

'Twas my sole island; there I dwelt alone—
  No customs-house, collector nor collection,
But a man came who in a pious tone
Condoled with me that I had never known
  The manifest advantage of Protection.

So when the trading-boat arrived one day
  He threw a stink-pot into its mid-section.
The traders paddled for their lives away,
Nor came again into that haunted bay,
  The blessed home thereafter of Protection.

Then down he sat, that philanthropic man,
  And spat upon some mud of his selection,
And worked it with his knuckles in a pan
To shapes of shells and coral things, and span
  A thread of song in glory of Protection.

He baked them in the sun.   His air devout
  Enchanted me.   I made a genuflexion:
"God help you, gentle sir," I said.   "No doubt,"
He answered gravely, "I'll get on without
  Assistance now that we have got Protection."

Thenceforth I bought his wares—at what a price
  For shells and corals of such imperfection!
"Ah, now," said he, "your lot is truly nice."
But still in all that isle there was no spice
  To season to my taste that dish, Protection.

SUBTERRANEAN PHANTASIES

I died.   As meekly in the earth I lay,
  With shriveled fingers reverently folded,
The worm—uncivil engineer!—my clay
  Tunneled industriously, and the mole did.
  My body could not dodge them, but my soul did;

For that had flown from this terrestrial ball
And I was rid of it for good and all.

So there I lay, debating what to do—
    What measures might most usefully be taken
To circumvent the subterranean crew
    Of anthropophagi and save my bacon.
    My fortitude was all the while unshaken,
But any gentleman, of course, protests
Against receiving uninvited guests.

However proud he might be of his meats,
    Not even Apicius, nor, I think, Lucullus,
Wasted on tramps his culinary sweets;
    "Aut Cæsar," say judicious hosts, *" aut nullus."*
    And though when Marcius came unbidden Tullus
Aufidius feasted him because he starved,
Marcius by Tullus afterward was carved.

We feed the hungry, as the book commands
    (For men might question else our orthodoxy)
But do not care to see the outstretched hands,
    And so we minister to them by proxy.
    When Want, in his improper person, knocks he
Finds we're engaged. The graveworm's very fresh
To think we like his presence in the flesh.

So, as I said, I lay in doubt; in all
  That underworld no judges could determine
My rights. When Death approaches them they fall,
  And falling, naturally soil their ermine.
  And still below ground, as above, the vermin
That work by dark and silent methods win
The case—the burial-case that one is in.

Cases at law so slowly get ahead,
  Even when the right is visibly unclouded,
That if all men are classed as quick and dead,
  The judges all are dead, though some unshrouded.
  Pray Jove that when they're actually crowded
On Styx's brink, and Charon rows in sight,
His bark prove worse than Cerberus's bite.

Ah! Cerberus, if you had but begot
  A race of three-mouthed dogs for man to nourish
And women to caress, the muse had not
  Lamented the decay of virtues currish,
  And triple-hydrophobia now would flourish.
For barking, biting, kissing to employ
Canine repeaters were indeed a joy.

Lord! how we cling to this vile world! Here I,
  Whose dust was laid ere I began this carping,
By moles and worms and such familiar fry

Run through and through, am singing still and harp-
    ing
Of mundane matters—flatting, too, and sharping.
I hate the Angel of the Sleeping-Cup:
So I'm for getting—and for shutting—up.

IN MEMORIAM

Beauty (they called her) wasn't a maid
Of many things in the world afraid.
She wasn't a maid who turned and fled
At sight of a mouse, alive or dead.
She wasn't a maid a man could "shoo"
By shouting, however abruptly, "Boo!"
She wasn't a maid who'd run and hide
If her face and figure you idly eyed.
She wasn't a maid who'd blush and shake
When asked what part of the fowl she'd take.
(I blush myself to confess she preferred,
And commonly got, the most of the bird.)
She wasn't a maid to simper because
She was asked to sing—if she ever was.
In short, if the truth must be displayed
All naked—Beauty wasn't a maid.

Beauty, furry and fine and fat,
Yawny and clawy, sleek and all that,
Was a pampered and spoiled Angora cat!
I loved her well, and I'm proud that she
Wasn't indifferent, quite, to me;
In fact I have sometimes gone so far
(You know, mesdames, how silly men are)
As to think she preferred—excuse the conceit—
My legs upon which to sharpen her feet.
Perhaps it shouldn't have counted for much,
But I started and thrilled beneath her touch!

Ah, well, that's ancient history now:
The fingers of Time have touched my brow,
And I hear with never a start to-day
That Beauty has passed from the earth away.
Gone!—her death-song (it killed her) sung.
Gone!—her fiddlestrings all unstrung.
Gone to the bliss of a new *régime*
Of turkey smothered in seas of cream;
Of roasted mice (a superior breed,
To science unknown and the coarser need
Of the living cat) cooked by the flame
Of the dainty soul of an erring dame
Who had given to purity all her care,
Neglecting the duty of daily prayer,—
Crisp, delicate mice, just touched with spice

By the ghost of a breeze from Paradise;
A very digestible sort of mice.

Let scoffers sneer, I purpose to hold
That Beauty has mounted the Stair of Gold,
To eat and eat, forever and aye,
On a velvet rug from a golden tray.
But the human spirit—that is my creed—
Rots in the ground like a barren seed.
That is my creed, abhorred by Man
But approved by Cat since time began.
Till Death shall kick at me, thundering "Scat!"
I shall hold to that, I shall hold to that.

THE STATESMEN

How blest the land that counts among
    Her sons so many good and wise,
To execute great feats of tongue
    When troubles rise.

Behold them mounting every stump,
    By speech our liberty to guard.
Observe their courage—see them jump,
    And come down hard!

"Walk up, walk up!" each cries aloud,
    "And learn from me what you must do
To turn aside the thunder cloud,
    The earthquake too.

"Beware the wiles of yonder quack
    Who stuffs the ears of all that pass.
I—I alone can show that black
    Is white as grass."

They shout through all the day and break
    The silence of the night as well.
They'd make—I wish they'd *go* and make—
    Of Heaven a Hell.

A advocates free silver, B
    Free trade and C free banking laws.
Free board, clothes, lodging would from me
    Win warm applause.

Lo, D lifts up his voice: "You see
    The single tax on land would fall
On all alike." More evenly
    No tax at all.

" With paper money," bellows E,
  " We'll all be rich as lords."   No doubt—
And richest of the lot will be
    The chap without.

As many " cures " as addle-wits
  Who know not what the ailment is!
Meanwhile the patient foams and spits
    Like a gin fizz.

Alas, poor Body Politic,
  Your fate is all too clearly read:
To be not altogether quick,
    Nor very dead.

You take your exercise in squirms,
  Your rest in fainting fits between.
'Tis plain that your disorder's worms—
    Worms fat and lean.

Worm Capital, Worm Labor dwell
  Within your maw and muscle's scope.
Their quarrels make your life a Hell,
    Your death a hope.

God send you find not such an end
  To ills however sharp and huge!

God send you convalesce! God send
  You vermifuge.

BROTHERS

SCENE—*A lawyer's dreadful den.*
Enter stall-fed citizen.

LAWYER.—Mornin'. How-de-do?
  CITIZEN. Sir, same to you.
Called as counsel to retain you
In a case that I'll explain you.
Sad, *so* sad! Heart almost broke.
Hang it! where's my kerchief? Smoke?
Brother, sir, and I, of late,
Came into a large estate.
Brother's—h'm, ha,—rather queer
Sometimes [*tapping forehead*] here.
What he needs—you know—a " writ "—
Something, eh? that will permit
Me to manage, sir, in fine,
His estate, as well as mine.
 Of course he'll storm; 'twill break, I fear,
His loving heart—excuse this tear.
  LAWYER.—Have you nothing more?
All of this you said before—

When last night I took your case.
    CITIZEN.—Why, sir, your face
Ne'er before has met my view!
    LAWYER.—Eh? The devil! True:
My mistake—it was your brother.
But you're very like each other.

THE CYNIC'S BEQUEST

In that fair city, Ispahan,
There dwelt a problematic man,
Whose angel never was released,
Who never once let out his beast,
But kept, through all the seasons' round,
Silence unbroken and profound.
No Prophecy, with ear applied
To key-hole of the future, tried
Successfully to catch a hint
Of what he'd do nor when begin't;
As sternly did his past defy
Mild Retrospection's backward eye.
Though all admired his silent ways,
The women loudest were in praise:
For ladies love those men the most
Who never, never, never boast—

Who ne'er disclose their aims and ends
To naughty, naughty, naughty friends.

Yet, sooth to say, the fame outran
The merit of this doubtful man,
For taciturnity in him,
Though not a mere caprice nor whim,
Was not a virtue, such as truth,
High birth, or beauty, wealth or youth.
'Twas known, indeed, throughout the span
Of Ispahan, of Gulistan—
These utmost limits of the earth
Knew that the man was dumb from birth.

Unto the Sun with deep salaams
The Parsee spreads his morning palms
(A beacon blazing on a height
Warms o'er his piety by night.)
The Moslem deprecates the deed,
Cuts off the head that holds the creed,
Then reverently goes to grass,
Muttering thanks to Balaam's Ass
For faith and learning to refute
Idolatry so dissolute!
But should a maniac dash past,
With straws in beard and hands upcast,
To him (through whom, whene'er inclined

To preach a bit to Madmankind,
The Holy Prophet speaks his mind)
Our True Believer lifts his eyes
Devoutly and his prayer applies;
But next to Solyman the Great
Reveres the idiot's sacred state.
Small wonder then, our worthy mute
Was held in popular repute.
Had he been blind as well as mum,
Been lame as well as blind and dumb,
No bard that ever sang or soared
Could say how he had been adored.
More meagerly endowed, he drew
An homage less prodigious.   True,
No soul his praises but did utter—
All plied him with devotion's butter,
But none had out—'twas to their credit—
The proselyting sword to spread it.
I state these truths, exactly why
The reader knows as well as I;
They've nothing in the world to do
With what I hope we're coming to
If Pegasus be good enough
To move when he has stood enough.
Egad! his ribs I would examine
Had I a sharper spur than famine,
Or even with that if 'twould incline

To examine his instead of mine.
Where was I? Ah, that silent man
Who dwelt one time in Ispahan.
He had a name—was known to all
As Meerza Solyman Zingall.

There lived afar in Astrabad,
A man the world agreed was mad,
So wickedly he broke his joke
Upon the heads of duller folk,
So miserly, from day to day,
He gathered up and hid away
In vaults obscure and cellars haunted
What many worthy people wanted.
A stingy man!—the tradesmen's palms
Were spread in vain: " I give no alms
Without inquiry "—so he'd say,
And beat the needy duns away.
The bastinado did, 'tis true,
Persuade him, now and then, a few
Odd tens of thousands to disburse
To glut the taxman's hungry purse,
But still, so rich he grew, his fear
Was constant that the Shah might hear.
(The Shah had heard it long ago,
And asked the taxman if 'twere so,

Who promptly answered, rather airish,
The man had long been on the parish.)
The more he feared, the more he grew
A cynic and a miser, too,
Until his bitterness and pelf
Made him a terror to himself;
Then, with a razor's neckwise stroke,
He tartly cut his final joke.
So perished, not an hour too soon,
The wicked Muley Ben Maroon.

From Astrabad to Ispahan
At camel-speed the rumor ran
That, breaking through tradition hoar,
And throwing all his kinsmen o'er,
The miser'd left his mighty store
Of gold—his palaces and lands—
To needy and deserving hands
(Except a penny here and there
To pay the dervishes for prayer.)
'Twas known indeed throughout the span
Of earth, and into Hindustan
That our beloved mute was the
Residuary legatee.
The people said 'twas very well,
And each man had a tale to tell

Of how he'd had a finger in't
By dropping many a friendly hint
At Astrabad, you see. But ah,
They feared the news would reach the Shah!

To prove the will, the lawyers bore't
Before the Kadi's awful court,
Who nodded, when he heard it read,
Confirmingly, his drowsy head,
Nor thought, his sleepiness so great,
Himself to gobble the estate.
"I give," the dead had writ, "my all
To Meerza Solyman Zingall
Of Ispahan. With this estate
I might quite easily create
Ten thousand ingrates, but I shun
Temptation and create but one,
In whom the whole unthankful crew
The rich man's air that ever drew
To fat their pauper lungs I fire
With vain vicarious desire!
From foul Ingratitude's base rout
I pick this hapless devil out,
Bestowing on him all my lands,
My treasures, camels, slaves and bands
Of wives—I give him all this loot,

And throw my blessing in to boot.
Behold, all men, in this bequest
Philanthropy's long wrongs redressed:
To speak me ill that man I dower
With fiercest will who lacks the power.
Allah il Allah! now let him bloat
With rancor till his heart's afloat,
Unable to discharge the wave
Upon his benefactor's grave!"

Forth in their wrath the people came
And swore it was a sin and shame
To trick their blessed mute; and each
Protested, serious of speech,
That though he'd long foreseen the worst
He'd been against it from the first.
By many means they vainly tried
The testament to set aside,
Each ready with his empty purse
To take upon himself the curse;
For *they* had powers of invective
Enough to make it ineffective.
The ingrates mustered, every man,
And marched in force to Ispahan
(Which had not quite accommodation)
And held a camp of indignation.

The man, this while, who never spoke—
On whom had fallen this thunder-stroke
Of fortune, gave no feeling vent,
Nor dropped a hint of his intent.
Whereas no power to him came
His benefactor to defame,
Some (such a length had slander gone to)
Even whispered that he didn't want to!
But none his secret could divine;
If suffering he made no sign
Until one night as winter neared
From all his haunts he disappeared—
Evanished in a doubtful blank
Like little crayfish in a bank,
Their heads retracting when you find 'em,
And pulling in their holes behind 'em.

All through the land of Gul, the stout
Young Spring is kicking Winter out.
The grass sneaks in upon the scene,
Defacing it with bottle-green.
The stumbling lamb arrives to ply
His restless tail in every eye,
Eats nasty mint to spoil his meat
And make himself unfit to eat.
His noisy throat the bulbul tears—
In every grove blasphemes and swears

As the immodest rose displays
Her shameless charms a dozen ways.
Lo! now, throughout the utmost span
Of Ispahan—of Gulistan—
A big new book's displayed in all
The shops and cumbers every stall.
The price is low—the dealers say 'tis—
And the rich are treated to it gratis.
Engraven on its foremost page
These title-words the eye engage:
" The Life of Muley Ben Maroon,
Of Astrabad—Rogue, Thief, Buffoon
And Miser—Liver by the Sweat
Of Better Men: A Lamponette
Composed in Rhyme and Written All
By Meerza Solyman Zingall!"

CORRECTED NEWS

'Twas a maiden lady, the newspapers say,
Pious and prim and a bit gone-gray.
  She slept like an angel, holy and white,
  Till ten o'clock in the shank o' the night,
When men and other wild animals prey,
And then she cried in the viewless gloom:
" There's a man in the room, a man in the room!"

And this maiden lady, they make it appear,
Leapt out of the window, five fathom sheer!

Alas, that lying is such a sin
When newspaper men need bread and gin
   And none can be had for less than a lie!
For the maiden lady a bit gone-gray
Saw the man in the room from across the way,
And leapt, not out of the window but in—
   Ten fathoms sheer, as I hope to die!

MR. FINK'S DEBATING DONKEY

Of a person known as Peters I will humbly crave your
      leave
An unusual adventure into narrative to weave—
Mr. William Perry Peters, of the town of Muscatel,
A public educator and an orator as well.
Mr. Peters had a weakness which, 'tis painful to relate,
Was a strong predisposition to the pleasures of debate.
He would foster disputation wheresoever he might be;
In polygonal contention none so happy was as he.
'Twas observable, however, that the exercises ran
Into monologue by Peters, that rhetorical young man.

And she Muscatelian rustics who assisted at the show,
By involuntary silence testified their overthrow—
Mr. Peters, all unheedful of their silence and their
    grief,
Still effacing every vestige of erroneous belief.
O, he was a sore affliction to all heretics so bold
As to entertain opinions that he didn't care to hold.

One day—'twas in pursuance of a pedagogic plan
For the mental elevation of Uncultivated Man—
Mr. Peters, to his pupils, in dismissing them, explained
That the Friday evening following (unless, indeed, it
    rained)
Would be signalized by holding in the schoolhouse a
    debate
Free to all who their opinions might desire to venti-
    late
On the question, " Which is better, as a serviceable gift,
Speech or hearing, from barbarity the human mind to
    lift? "
The pupils told their fathers, who, forehanded always,
    met
At the barroom to discuss it every evening, dry or wet.
They argued it and argued it and spat upon the stove,
And the non-committal barman on their differences
    throve.
And I state it as a maxim in a loosish kind of way:

You'll have the more to back your word the less you
    have to say.
Public interest was lively, but one Ebenezer Fink
Of the Rancho del Jackrabbit, only seemed to sit and
    think.

On the memorable evening all the men of Muscatel
Came to listen to the logic and the eloquence as well—
All but William Perry Peters, whose attendance there,
    I fear,
Was to wreak his ready rhetoric upon the public ear,
And prove (whichever side he took) that hearing
    wouldn't lift
The human mind as ably as the other, greater gift.
The judges being chosen and the disputants enrolled,
The question he proceeded *in extenso* to unfold:
"*Resolved*—The sense of hearing lifts the mind up out
    of reach
Of the fogs of error better than the faculty of speech."
This simple proposition he expounded, word by word,
Till they best understood it who least perfectly had
    heard.
Even the judges comprehended what he ventured to ex-
    plain—
The impact of a spit-ball admonishing in vain.
Beginning at a period before Creation's morn,

He had reached the bounds of tolerance and Adam yet
  unborn.

As down the early centuries of pre-historic time

He tracked important principles and quoted striking
  rhyme,

And Whisky Bill, prosaic soul! proclaiming him a jay,

Had risen and like an earthquake, "reeled unheededly
  away,"

And a late lamented cat, when opportunity should
  serve,

Was preparing to embark upon her parabolic curve,

A noise arose outside—the door was opened with a
  bang,

And old Ebenezer Fink was heard ejaculating
  " G'lang! "

Straight into that assembly gravely marched without a
  wink

An ancient ass—the property it was of Mr. Fink.

Its ears depressed and beating time to its infestive
  tread,

Silent through silence, moved amain that stately quad-
  ruped!

It stopped before the orator, and in the lamplight thrown

Upon its tail they saw that member weighted with a
  stone.

Then spake old Ebenezer: " Gents, I heern o' this debate

On w'ether v'ice or y'ears is best the mind to elevate.

Now 'yer's a bird ken throw some light uponto that tough theme:

He has 'em both, I'm free to say, oncommonly extreme.

He wa'n't invited for to speak, but he will not refuse

(If t'other gentleman ken wait) to exposay his views."

Ere merriment or anger o'er amazement could prevail,

He cut the string that held the stone on that canary's tail.

Freed from the weight, that member made a gesture of delight,

Then rose until its rigid length was horizontal quite.

With lifted head and level ears along his withers laid,

Jack sighed, refilled his lungs and then—to put it mildly —brayed!

He brayed until the stones were stirred in circumjacent hills,

And sleeping women rose and fled, in divers kinds of frills.

'Tis said that awful bugle-blast—to make the story brief—

Wafted William Perry Peters through the window, like a leaf!

Such is the tale. If anything additional occurred

'Tis not set down, though, truly, I remember to have heard

That a gentleman named Peters, now residing at Soquel,
A considerable distance from the town of Muscatel,
Is opposed to education, and to rhetoric, as well.

TO MY LAUNDRESS

Saponacea, wert thou not so fair
  I'd curse thee for thy multitude of sins—
  For sending home my clothes all full of pins,
A shirt occasionally that's a snare
And a delusion, got, the Lord knows where,
  The Lord knows why, a sock whose outs and ins
  None know, nor where it ends nor where begins,
And fewer cuffs than ought to be my share.
But when I mark thy lilies how they grow,
  And the red roses of thy ripening charms,
    I bless the lovelight in thy dark eyes dreaming.
I'll never pay thee, but I'd gladly go
  Into the magic circle of thine arms,
    Supple and fragrant from repeated steaming.

FAME

One thousand years I slept beneath the sod,
　My sleep in 1901 beginning,
Then, by the action of some scurvy god
　Who happened then to recollect my sinning,
　I was revived and given another inning.
On breaking from my grave I saw a crowd—
　A formless multitude of men and women,
Gathered about a ruin. Clamors loud
　I heard, and curses deep enough to swim in;
　And, pointing at me, one said: " Let's put *him* in! "
Then each turned on me with an evil look,
As in my ragged shroud I stood and shook.

" Nay, good Posterity," I cried, " forbear!
　If that's a jail I fain would be remaining
Outside, for truly I should little care
　To catch my death of cold. I'm just regaining
　The life lost long ago by my disdaining
To take precautions against draughts like those
　That, haply, penetrate that cracked and splitting
Old structure." Then an aged wight arose
　From a chair of state in which he had been sitting,
　And with preliminary coughing, spitting
And wheezing, said: " 'Tis not a jail, we're sure,
Whate'er it may have been when it was newer.

" 'Twas found two centuries ago, o'ergrown
   With brush and ivy, all undoored, ungated;
And in restoring it we found a stone
   Set here and there in the dilapidated
   And crumbling frieze, inscribed, in antiquated
Big characters, with certain uncouth names,
   Which we conclude were borne of old by awful
Rapscallions guilty of all sinful games—
   Vagrants engaged in practices unlawful,
   And orators less sensible than jawful.
So each ten years we add to the long row
A name, the most unworthy that we know."

" But why," I asked, " put mine in? " He replied·
   " You look it "—and the judgment pained me greatly;
Right gladly would I then and there have died,
   But that I'd risen from the grave so lately.
   But on examining that solemn, stately
Old ruin I remarked: " My friends, you err—
   The truth of this is just what I expected.
This building in its time made quite a stir.
   I lived (was famous, too) when 'twas erected.
   The names here first inscribed were much respected.
This is the Hall of Fame, or I'm a stork,
And this goat-pasture once was called New York."

OMNES VANITAS

Alas for ambition's possessor!
  Alas for the famous and proud!
The Isle of Manhattan's best dresser
  Is wearing a hand-me-down shroud.

The world has forgotten his glory;
  The wagoner sings on his wain,
And Chauncey Depew tells a story,
  And jackasses laugh in the lane.

CONSOLATION

Little's the good to sit and grieve
Because the serpent tempted Eve.
Better to wipe your eyes and take
A club and go out and kill a snake.

But if you prefer, as I suspect,
To philosophize, why, then, reflect:
If the cunning rascal upon the limb
Hadn't tempted her she'd have tempted him.

FATE

Alas, alas, for the tourist's guide!—
He turned from the beaten trail aside,
Wandered bewildered, lay down and died.

O grim is the Irony of Fate:
It switches the man of low estate
And loosens the dogs upon the great.

It lights the fireman to roast the cook;
The fisherman writhes upon the hook,
And the flirt is slain with a tender look.

The undertaker it overtakes;
It saddles the cavalier, and makes
The haughtiest butcher into steaks.

Assist me, gods, to balk the decree!
Nothing I'll do and nothing I'll be,
In order that nothing be done to me.

PHILOSOPHER BIMM

Republicans think Jonas Bimm
A Democrat gone mad,
And Democrats consider him
Republican and bad.

The Lout reviles him as a Dude
 And gives it him right hot;
The Dude condemns his crassitude
 And calls him *sans-culottes.*

Derided as an Anglophile
 By Anglophobes, forsooth,
As Anglophobe he feels, the while,
 The Anglophilic tooth.

The Churchman calls him Atheist;
 The Atheists, rough-shod,
Have ridden o'er him long and hissed:
 "The wretch believes in God!"

The Saints whom clergymen we call
 Would kill him if they could;
The Sinners (scientists and all)
 Complain that he is good.

All men deplore the difference
 Between themselves and him,
And all devise expedients
 For paining Jonas Bimm.

I too, with wild demoniac glee,
 Would put out both his eyes;

For Mr. Bimm appears to me
  Insufferably wise!

REMINDED

Beneath my window twilight made
Familiar mysteries of shade.
Faint voices from the darkening down
Were calling vaguely to the town.

Intent upon a low, far gleam
That burned upon the world's extreme,
I sat, with short reprieve from grief,
And turned the volume, leaf by leaf,
Wherein a hand long dead had wrought
A million miracles of thought.
My fingers carelessly unclung
The lettered pages, and among
Them wandered witless, nor divined
The wealth in which, poor fools, they mined.
The soul that should have led their quest
Was dreaming in the level west,
Where a tall tower, stark and still,
Uplifted on a distant hill,
Stood lone and passionless to claim
Its guardian star's returning flame.

I know not how my dream was broke,
But suddenly my spirit woke
Filled with a foolish fear to look
Upon the hand that clove the book,
Significantly pointing; next
I bent attentive to the text,
And read—and as I read grew old—
The mindless words: "Poor Tom's a-cold!"

Ah me! to what a subtle touch
The brimming cup resigns its clutch
Upon the wine. Dear God, is't writ
That hearts their overburden bear
Of bitterness though thou permit
The pranks of Chance, alurk in nooks,
And striking coward blows from books,
And dead hands reaching everywhere?

SALVINI IN AMERICA

Come, gentlemen—your gold.
  Thanks; welcome to the show,
To hear a story told
  In words you do not know.

Now, great Salvini, rise
　　And thunder through your tears!
Aha! friends, let your eyes
　　Interpret to your ears.

Gods! 'tis a goodly game.
　　Observe his stride—how grand!
When legs like his declaim
　　Who can misunderstand?

See how that arm goes round.
　　It says, as plain as day:
" I love," " The lost is found,"
　　" Well met, sir," or, " Away! "

And mark the drawing down
　　Of brows. How accurate
The language of that frown:
　　Pain, gentlemen—or hate.

Those of the critic trade
　　Swear it is all as clear
As if his tongue were made
　　To fit an English ear.

Hear that Italian phrase!
　　Greek to your sense, 'tis true:

But shrug, expression, gaze—
   Well, they are Grecian too.

But it is Art! God wot
   Art's tongue to all is known.
Faith! he to whom 'twere not
   Would better hold his own.

Shakespeare says act and word
   Should match together true.
For what you've seen and heard,
   How can you doubt they do?

Enchanting drama! Mark
   The crowd " from pit to dome ";
One box alone is dark—
   The prompter stays at home.

Stupendous artist! You
   Are lord of joy and woe:
We thrill if you say " Boo,"
   And thrill if you say " Bo."

ANOTHER WAY

I lay in silence, dead. A woman came
  And laid a rose upon my breast and said:
" May God be merciful." She spoke my name,
  And added: " It is strange to think him dead.

" He loved me well enough, but 'twas his way
  To speak it lightly." Then, beneath her breath:
" Besides "—I knew what further she would say,
  But then a footfall broke my dream of death.

To-day the words are mine. I lay the rose
  Upon her breast, and speak her name, and 'deem
It strange indeed that she is dead. God knows
  I had more pleasure in the other dream.

ART

For Gladstone's portrait five thousand pounds
  Were paid. 'tis said, to Sir John Millais.
  I cannot help thinking that such fine pay
Transcended reason's uttermost bounds.

For it seems to me uncommonly queer
That a painted British statesman's price
Exceeds the established value thrice
Of a living statesman over here.

TO ONE ACROSS THE WAY

When at your window radiant you've stood
I've sometimes felt—forgive me if I erred—
That some slight thought of me perhaps has stirred
Your heart to beat less gently than it should.
I know you beautiful; that you are good
I hope—or fear—I cannot choose the word,
Nor rightly suit it to the thought. I've heard
Reason at love's dictation never could.
Blindly to this dilemma so I grope,
As one whose every pathway has a snare:
If you are minded in the saintly fashion
Of your pure face my passion's without hope;
If not, alas! I equally despair,
For what to me were hope without the passion?

TO A DEBTOR ABROAD

Grief for an absent lover, husband, friend,
Is barely felt before it comes to end:
A score of early consolations serve
To modify its mouth's dejected curve;
But woes of creditors when debtors flee
Forever swell the separating sea.
When standing on an alien shore you mark
The steady course of some intrepid bark,
How sweet to think a tear for you abides,
Not all unuseful, in the wave she rides!—
That sighs for you commingle in the gale
Beneficently bellying her sail!

GENESIS

God said: " Let there be Man," and from the clay
Adam came forth and, thoughtful, walked away.
The matrix whence his body was obtained,
An empty, man-shaped cavity, remained
All unregarded from that early time
Till in a recent storm it filled with slime.
Now Satan, envying the Master's power
To make the meat himself could but devour,

Strolled to the place and, standing by the pool,
Exerted all his will to make a fool.
A miracle!—from out that ancient hole
Rose Doxey, lacking nothing but a soul.
" To give him that I've not the power divine,"
Said Satan, sadly, "but I'll lend him mine."
He breathed it into him, a vapor black,
And to this day has never got it back.

LIBERTY

" 'Let there be Liberty!' God said, and lo!
The skies were red and luminous. The glow
    Struck first Columbia's kindling mountain peaks
One hundred and eleven years ago! "

So sang a patriot whom once I saw
Descending Bunker's holy hill. With awe
    I noted that he shone with sacred light,
Like Moses with the tables of the Law.

One hundred and eleven years? O small
And paltry period compared with all
    The tide of centuries that flowed and ebbed
To etch Yosemite's divided wall!

Ah, Liberty, they sing you always young
Whose harps are in your adoration strung.
   (Each swears you are his countrywoman, too,
And speak no language but his mother tongue.)

And truly, lass, although with shout and horn
Man has all-hailed you from creation's morn
   I cannot think you old—I think, indeed,
You are by twenty centuries unborn.

THE PASSING OF SHEPHERD

The sullen church-bell's intermittent moan,
The dirge's melancholy monotone,
The measured march, the drooping flags, attest
A great man's progress to his place of rest.
Along broad avenues himself decreed
To serve his fellow men's disputed need—
Past parks he raped away from robbers' thrift
And gave to poverty, wherein to lift
Its voice to curse the giver and the gift—
Past noble structures that he reared for men
To meet in and revile him, tongue and pen,
Draws the long retinue of death to show
The fit credentials of a proper woe.

"Boss" Shepherd, you are dead. Your hand no
    more
Throws largess to the mobs that ramp and roar
For blood of benefactors who disdain
Their purity of purpose to explain,
Their righteous motive and their scorn of gain.
Your period of dream—'twas but a breath—
Is closed in the indifference of death.
Sealed in your silences, to you alike
If hands are lifted to applaud or strike,
No more to your dull, inattentive ear
Praise of to-day than curse of yesteryear.
From the same lips the honied phrases fall
That still are bitter from cascades of gall.
We note the shame; you in your depth of dark
The red-writ testimony cannot mark
On every honest cheek; your senses all
Locked, incomunicado, in your pall,
Know not who sit and blush, who stand and bawl.

"Seven Grecian cities claim great Homer dead,
Through which the living Homer begged his
    bread."
"Neglected genius!"—that is sad indeed,
But malice better would ignore than heed,
And Shepherd's soul, we rightly may suspect,
Prayed often for the mercy of neglect

OF AMBROSE BIERCE 199

When hardly did he dare to leave his door
Without a guard behind him and before
To save him from the gentlemen that now
In cheap and easy reparation bow
Heads hypocritical above his corse
To counterfeit a grief that's half remorse.

The pageant passes and the exile sleeps,
And well his silent tongue the secret keeps
Of the great peace he found afar, until,
Death's writ of extradition to fulfill,
They brought him helpless, from that friendly
　　zone
To be a show and pastime in his own—
A final opportunity to those
Who fling with equal aim the stone and rose;
That at the living till his soul is freed,
This at the body to conceal the deed!

Lone on his hill he's lying to await
What added honors may befit his state—
The monument, the statue, or the arch
(Where knaves may come to weep and dupes to
　　march)
Builded by clowns to brutalize the scenes
His genius beautified.　To get the means,

His newly good traducers all are dunned
For contributions to the conscience fund.
If each subscribe (and pay) one cent 'twill rear
A structure taller than their tallest ear.
1903.

TO MAUDE

Not as two errant spheres together grind
　　With monstrous ruin in the vast of space,
　　Destruction born of that malign embrace,
Their hapless peoples all to 'death consigned—
Not so when our intangible worlds of mind,
　　Even mine and yours, each with its spirit race,
　　Of beings shadowy in form and face,
Shall drift together on some blessed wind.
No, in that marriage of gloom and light
　　All miracles of beauty shall be wrought,
　　　Attesting a diviner faith than man's;
For all my sad-eyed daughters of the night
　　Shall smile on your sweet seraphim of thought,
　　　Nor any jealous god forbid the banns.

THE BIRTH OF VIRTUE

When, long ago, the young world circling flew
Through wider reaches of a richer blue,
New-eyed, the men and maids saw, manifest,
The thoughts untold in one another's breast—
Each wish displayed, and every passion learned;
A look revealed them as a look discerned.
But sating Time with clouds o'ercast their eyes;
Desire was hidden, and the lips framed lies.
A goddess then, emerging from the dust,
Fair Virtue rose, the daughter of Distrust.

THE SCURRIL PRESS

Tom Jonesmith (*loquitur*) : I've slept right through
The night—a rather clever thing to do.
How soundly women sleep [*looks at his wife*].
They're all alike.   The sweetest thing in life
Is woman when she lies with folded tongue,
Its toil completed and its day-song sung.
[*Thump!*]   That's the morning paper.   What a bore
That it should be delivered at the door.
There ought to be some expeditious way
To get it *to* one.   By this long delay

The fizz gets off the news [*a rap is heard*].
That's Jane, the housemaid; she's an early bird;
She's brought it to the bedroom door, good soul.
[*Gets up and takes it in.*]   Upon the whole,
The system's not so bad a one.   What's here?
Gad! if they've not got after—listen, dear,
[*To sleeping wife*]—young Gastrotheos.   **Well,**
If Freedom shrieked when Kosciusko fell
She'll shriek again—with laughter—seeing how
They treated Gast. with her.   Yet I'll allow
'Tis right if he goes dining at The Pup
With Mrs. Thing.

              WIFE [*briskly, waking up*]:
With her?   The hussy!   Yes, it serves him right.

    JONESMITH [*continuing to "seek the light"*]:
What's this about old Impycu?   That's good!
Grip—that's the funny man—says Impy should
Be used as a decoy in shooting tramps.
I knew old Impy when he had the "**stamps**"
To buy us all out, and he wasn't then
So bad a chap to have about.   Grip's pen
Is just a tickler!—and the world, no **doubt,**
Is better with it than it was without.
What? thirteen ladies—Jumping Jove! we **know**
Them nearly all!—who gamble at a low
And very shocking game of cards called "draw"!
O **cracky**, how they'll squirm! ha-ha! haw-haw!

Let's see what else [*wife snores*]. Well, I'll be blest!
A woman doesn't understand a jest.
Hello! What, what? the scurvy wretch proceeds
To take a fling at *me*, condemn him! [*reads*] :
Tom Jonesmith—my name's Thomas, vulgar cad!—
Of the new Shavings Bank—the man's gone mad!
That's libelous; I'll have him up for that—
Has had his corns cut. Devil take the rat!
What business is't of his, I'd like to know?
He didn't have to cut them. Gods! what low
And scurril things our papers have become!
You skim their contents and you get but scum.
Here, Mary [*waking wife*] I've been attacked
In this vile sheet. By Jove, it is a fact!

WIFE [*reading it*] : How wicked! Who do you
Suppose 'twas wrote it?

JONESMITH : Who? why, who
But Grip, the so-called funny-man—he wrote
Me up because I'd not discount his note.
[*Blushes like sunset at the hideous lie—*
He'll think of one that's better by and by;
Throws down the paper on the floor, and treads
A merry measure on it; kicks the shreds
And patches all about the room, and still
Performs his jig with unabated will.]

WIFE [*warbling sweetly, like an Elfland horn*] :
Dear, do be careful of that second corn.

STANLEY

Noting some great man s composition vile:
A head of wisdom and a heart of guile,
A will to conquer and a soul to dare,
Joined to the manners of a dancing bear,
Fools unaccustomed to the wide survey
Of various Nature's compensating sway;
Untaught to separate the wheat and chaff,
To praise the one and at the other laugh;
Yearn all in vain and impotently seek
Some flawless hero upon whom to wreak
The sycophantic worship of the weak.

Not so the wise, from superstition free,
Who find small pleasure in the supple knee;
Quick to discriminate 'twixt good and bad,
And willing in the king to find the cad—
No reason seen why genius and 'deceit,
The power to dazzle and the will to cheat,
The love of daring and the love of gin,
Should not dwell, peaceful, in a single skin.

To such, great Stanley, you're a hero still,
Despite your cradling in a tub for swill.

Your peasant manners can't efface the mark
Of light you drew across the Land of Dark.
In you the extremes of character are wed,
To serve the quick and vilify the dead.
Hero and clown! O, man of many sides,
The Muse of Truth adores you and derides,
And sheds, impartial, the revealing ray
Upon your head of gold and feet of clay.

ONE OF THE UNFAIR SEX

She stood at the ticket-seller's
   Serenely removing her glove,
While hundreds of strugglers and yellers,
   And some that were good at a shove,
   Were clustered behind her like bats in
    a cave and dissembling their love.

At night she still stood at that window
   Endeavoring her money to reach;
The crowds in her rear, how they sinned—O,
   How dreadfully sinned in their speech!
   Ten miles and a fraction extended their
    line, the historians teach.

She stands there to-day—legislation
   Has failed to remove her. The trains
No longer pull up at that station;
   And over the ghastly remains
     Of the army that waited and died of old
     age fall the snows and the rains.

THE LORD'S PRAYER ON A COIN

Upon this quarter-eagle's leveled face,
The Lord's Prayer, legibly inscribed, I trace.
"Our Father which "—the pronoun there is funny,
And shows the scribe to have addressed the money—
"Which art in Heaven "—an error this, no doubt:
The preposition should be stricken out.
Needless to quote; I only have designed
To praise the frankness of the pious mind
Which thought it natural and right to join,
With rare significancy, prayer and coin.

AD ABSURDUM

Congressman Rixey, you're a statesman—you
   Yourself will hardly say that you are not;
And yet I know not what you hope to do
   For those Confederates whose luckless lot
   Is to have lived through storms of Yankee shot

To this our day. They draw their breath, indeed,
   But from the Government no cent of what
So admirably serves your nobler need.
You work for it? Why, that all cavilers concede.

You'd call these " rebels " to the Soldiers' Homes
   On equal terms with persons whom they fought!
Whereat the " truly loyal " statesman foams
   At the loud mouth of him. But that is
      naught—
   He foams, not for he must, but for he ought:
For the Poll-patriot's emotions flow
   By taking (with much else of value)
      thought.
His feelings, if he have them, never blow
His cooling coal of anger to a brighter glow.

Well, well, sir, even the Devil may be right
   Through ignorance or accident. 'Tis said
We're sometimes dazzled with too great a light,
   In which the blind, with customary tread
   (And by a small, unblinking puppy led)
Walk prosperous courses to appointed goals.
   And so your critics, though without a head
Among them—eyeless, therefore, as the moles—
May wiser be than you, who damn their little
      souls!

If of two aged Southern gentlemen
Of equal need and worth, the one that tried
To cook the country's goose—or say its hen—
Be blest with all the cheer we can provide,
And which to t'other sternly is denied
Because he didn't, it will seem right queer.
The gods are logical and may deride.
Respect the Southern veteran, but fear
The laughter of Olympus sounding loud and
clear!

SAITH THE CZAR

My people come to me and make their moan:
"We starve, your Majesty—give us a stone."
That's flat rebellion!—how the devil dare
They starve right in my capital? Their prayer
For something in their bellies I will meet
With that which I'll not trouble them to eat.
They ask for greater freedom. No, indeed—
What happened to my ancestor who freed
The serfs? His grateful subjects duly flung
Something that spoke to him without a tongue.
So he was sacrificed for Freedom's sake,
And gathered to his fathers with a rake.
I from Autocracy my people free?
Ah, would to Heaven they could deliver me!

THE ROYAL JESTER

Once on a time, so ancient poets sing,
There reigned in Godknowswhere a certain king.
So great a monarch ne'er before was seen:
He was a hero, even to his queen,
In whose respect he held so high a place
That none had higher,—nay, not even the ace.
He was so just his parliament declared
Those subjects happy whom his laws had spared;
So wise that none of the debating throng
Had ever lived to prove him in the wrong;
So good that Crime his anger never feared,
And Beauty boldly plucked him by the beard;
So brave that if his army got a beating
None dared to face him when he was retreating.

This monarch kept a fool to make his mirth,
And loved him tenderly despite his worth.
Prompted by what caprice I cannot say,
He called the Fool before the throne one day
And to that minion seriously said:
"I'll abdicate, and you shall reign instead,
While I, attired in motley, will make sport
To entertain your Majesty and Court."

'Twas done and the Fool governed. He decreed
The time of harvest and the time of seed;
Ordered the rains and made the weather clear,
And had a famine every second year;
Altered the calendar to suit his freak,
Ordaining six whole holidays a week;
Religious creeds and sacred books prepared;
Made war when angry and made peace when scared.
New taxes he imposed; new laws he made;
Drowned those who broke them, who observed them,
    flayed.
In short, he ruled so well that all who'd not
Been starved, decapitated, hanged or shot
Made the whole country with his praises ring,
Declaring he was every inch a king;
And the High Priest averred 'twas very odd
If one so competent were not a god.

Meantime, his master, now in motley clad,
Wore such a visage, woful, wan and sad,
That some condoled with him as with a brother
Who, having lost a wife, had got another.
Others, mistaking his profession, often
Approached him to be measured for a coffin.
For years this highborn Jester never broke
The silence—he was pondering a joke.

At last, one day, in cap and bells arrayed,
He strode into the Council and displayed
A long bright smile, that glittered in the gloom
Like a gilt epitaph within a tomb.
Poising his bauble like a leader's staff,
To give the signal when (and why) to laugh,
He brought it down with peremptory stroke
And simultaneously cracked his joke!

I can't repeat it, friends. I ne'er could school
Myself to quote from any other fool:
A jest, if it were worse than mine, would start
My tears; if better, it would break my heart.
So, if you please, I'll hold you but to state
That royal Jester's melancholy fate.

The insulted nation, so the story goes,
Rose as one man—the very dead arose,
Springing indignant from the riven tomb,
And babes unborn leapt swearing from the womb!
All to the Council Chamber clamoring went,
By rage distracted and on vengeance bent.
In that vast hall, in due disorder laid,
The tools of legislation were displayed,
And the wild populace, its wrath to sate,
Seized them and heaved them at the Jester's pate.

Mountains of writing paper; pools and seas
Of ink awaiting, to become decrees,
Royal approval—and the same in stacks
Lay ready for attachment, backed with wax;
Pens to make laws, erasers to amend them,
With mucilage convenient to extend them;
Scissors for limiting their application,
Trash-baskets to repeal all legislation—
These, flung as missiles till the air was dense,
Were most offensive weapons of offense,
And by their aid the man was nigh destroyed.
They ne'er had been so harmlessly employed.
Whelmed underneath a load of legal cap,
His mouth egurgitating ink on tap,
His eyelids mucilaginously sealed,
His fertile head by scissors made to yield
Abundant harvestage of ears, his pelt,
In every wrinkle and on every welt,
Quickset with pencil-points from feet to gills
And thickly studded with a pride of quills,
The royal Jester in the dreadful strife
Was made (in short) an editor for life!

An idle tale, and yet a moral lurks
In this as plainly as in greater works.
I shall not give it birth: one moral here
Would die of loneliness within a year.

A CAREER IN LETTERS

When Liberverm resigned the chair
Of This or That in college, where
Two decades he had gorged his brain
With more than it could well contain,
In order to relieve the stress
He took to writing for the press.
Then Pondronummus said: " I'll help
This mine of talent to devel'p: "
And straightway bought with coin and credit
The *Thundergust* for him to edit.

The great man seized the pen and ink
And wrote so hard he couldn't think.
Ideas grew beneath his fist
And flew like falcons from his wrist.
His pen shot sparks all kinds of ways
Till all the rivers were ablaze,
And where the coruscations fell
Men uttered words I dare not spell.

Eftsoons with corrugated brow,
Wet towels bound about his pow,
Locked legs and failing appetite,
He thought so hard he couldn't write.

His soaring fancies, chickenwise,
Came home to roost and wouldn't rise.
With dimmer light and milder heat
His goose-quill staggered o'er the sheet,
Then dragged, then stopped; the finish came—
He couldn't even write his name.
The *Thundergust* in three short weeks
Had risen, roared, and split its cheeks.
Said Pondronummus, "How unjust!
The storm I raised has laid my dust!"

When, Moneybagger, you have aught
Invested in a vein of thought,
Be sure you've purchased not, instead,
That salted claim, a bookworm's head.

THE FOLLOWING PAIR

O very remarkable mortal,
  What food is engaging your jaws
And staining with amber their portal?
  "It's 'baccy I chaws."

And why do you sway in your walking,
  To right and left many degrees,

And hitch up your trousers when talking?
  " I follers the seas."

Great indolent shark in the rollers,
  Is " 'baccy," too, one of your faults?—
You, too, display maculate molars.
    " I dines upon salts."

Strange diet!—intestinal pain it
  Is commonly given to nip.
And how can you ever obtain it?
    " I follers the ship."

POLITICAL ECONOMY

" I beg you to note," said a Man to a Goose,
As he plucked from her bosom the plumage all loose,
" That pillows and cushions of feathers, and beds
As warm as maids' hearts and as soft as their heads,
Increase of life's comforts the general sum—
Which raises the standard of living." " Come, come,"
The Goose said impatiently, " tell me or cease,
How that is of any advantage to geese."
" What, what ! " said the man—" you are very obtuse !
Consumption no profit to those who produce?

No good to accrue to Supply from a grand
Progressive expansion, all around, of Demand?
Luxurious habits no benefit bring
To those who purvey the luxurious thing?
Consider, I pray you, my friend, how the growth
Of luxury promises—" "Promises," quoth
The sufferer, " what?—to what course is it pledged
To pay me for being so often defledged?"
" Accustomed "—this notion the plucker expressed
As he ripped out a handful of down from her breast—
" To one kind of luxury, people soon yearn
For others and ever for others in turn.
The man who to-night on your feathers will rest,
His mutton or bacon or beef to digest,
His hunger to-morrow will wish to assuage
With goose and a dressing of onions and sage."

THE UNPARDONABLE SIN

I reckon that ye never knew,
That dandy slugger, Tom Carew.
He had a touch as light an' free
As that of any honey-bee;
But where it lit there wasn't much
To jestify another touch.

O, what a Sunday-school it was
To watch him puttin' up his paws
An' roominate upon their heft—
Particular his holy left!
Tom was my style—that's all I say;
Some others may be equal gay.
What's come of him? Dunno, I'm sure;
He's dead—which makes his fate obscure.
I only started in to clear
One vital p'int in his career,
Which is to say—afore he died
He soiled his erming mighty snide.
Ye see he took to politics
And learnt them statesmen-fellers' tricks;
Pulled wires, wore stovepipe hats, used scent,
Just like he was the President;
Went to the Legislater; spoke
Right out agin the British yoke—
But that was right. He let his hair
Grow long to qualify for Mayor,
An' once or twice he poked his snoot
In Congress like a low galoot!
It had to come—no gent can hope
To wrastle God agin the rope.
Tom went from bad to wuss. Being dead,
I s'pose it oughtn't to be said,
For sech inikities as flow
From politics ain't fit to know.

But, if you think it's actin' white
To tell it—Thomas throwed a fight!

INDUSTRIAL DISCONTENT

As time rolled on the whole world came to be
    A desolation and a darksome curse;
And some one said: " The changes that you see
    In the fair frame of things, from bad to worse,
Are wrought by strikes. The sun withdrew his glim-
        mer
Because the moon assisted with her shimmer.

" Then, when poor Luna, straining very hard,
    Doubled her light to serve a darkling world,
He called her ' scab,' and meanly would retard
    Her rising: and at last the villain hurled
A heavy beam which knocked her o'er the Lion
Into the nebula of great O'Ryan.

" The planets all had struck some time before,
    Demanding what they said were equal rights:
Some pointing out that others had far more
    Than a fair dividend of satellites.
So all went out—but those the best provided,
If they had dared would rather have abided.

" The stars struck too—I think it was because
    The comets had more liberty than they,
And were not bound by any hampering laws,
    While *they* were fixed; and there are those who
        say
The comets' tresses nettled poor Antares,
A bald old orb, whose disposition varies.

" The earth's the only one that isn't in
    The movement—I suppose because she's watched
With horror and disgust how her fair skin
    Her pranking parasites have fouled and blotched
With blood and grease in every labor riot,
When seeing any purse or throat to fly at."

TEMPORA MUTANTUR

" The world is dull," I cried in my despair:
" Its myths and fables are no longer fair.

" Roll back thy centuries, O Father Time:
To Greece transport me in her golden prime.

" Give back the beautiful old gods again—
    The sportive Nymphs, the Dryad's jocund
        train,

" Pan piping on his reeds, the Naiades,
The Sirens singing by the sleepy seas.

" Nay, show me but a Gorgon and I'll dare
To lift mine eyes to her peculiar hair

"(The fatal horrors of her snaky pate,
That stiffen men into a stony state)

" And die—becoming, as my spirit flies,
A noble statue of myself, life size."

Straight as I spoke I heard the voice of Fate:
" Look up, my lad, the Gorgon sisters wait."

Lifting my eyes, I saw Medusa stand,
Stheno, Euryale, on either hand.

I gazed unpetrified and unappalled—
The girls had aged and were entirely bald!

A FALSE ALARM

When Gertrude Atherton pronounced the ladies
Of fair Manhattan hideous as Hades—
In eyes no splendor, and in cheeks no roses,
And, O ye godlings! rudimentary noses—

To pass a bad half-hour before their glasses,
Straight to their dressing-rooms ran dames and
    lasses,
Who, still dissenting from her curst appraisal,
Grew more pugnacious, but not less pugnasal.
Ladies, be calm: there's nothing to distress you—
The Sacred Englishman will rise and bless you.
No noses—none to speak of—is alarming,
But that you can't speak *through* them—that is
    charming!

CONTENTMENT

Sleep fell upon my senses and I dreamed
    Long years had circled since my life had fied.
The world was different, and all things seemed
    Remote and strange, like noises to the dead.
    And one great Voice there was; and some one said:
" Posterity is speaking—rightly deemed
Infallible "; and so I gave attention,
Hoping Posterity my name would mention.

" Illustrious Spirit," said the Voice, " appear!
    While we confirm eternally thy fame,
Before our dread tribunal answer, here,

Why do no statues celebrate thy name,
No monuments thy services proclaim?
Why did not thy contemporaries rear
To thee some schoolhouse or memorial college?
It looks almighty queer, you must acknowledge."

Up spake I hotly: "That is where you err!"
    But some one thundered in my ear: "You shan't
Be interrupting these proceedings, sir;
    The question was addressed to General Grant."
    Some other things were spoken which I can't
Distinctly now recall, but I infer,
By certain flushings of my cheek and forehead,
Posterity's environment is torrid.

Then heard I (this was in a dream, remark)
    Another Voice, clear, comfortable, strong,
As Grant's great shade, replying from the dark,
    Said in a tone that rang the earth along,
    And thrilled the senses of the judges' throng:
" I'd rather you would question why, in park
And street, my monuments were not erected
Than why they were." Then, waking, I reflected.
    1885.

CONSTANCY

I had a dream. A throng of people sped
Hard after something that before them fled—
    A ball that leapt and bounded. I pursued,
Kicking, like all the rest, at Bryan's head.

Ah, God, it was indeed a ghastly play!
That noble head—its locks in disarray
    Streaming like feathers of a shuttlecock—
Urged with resounding buffets on its way.

Ever the foremost in the chase accurst
Ran Two who in his life, too, had been first
    Among his followers. "Behold," I cried,
"Those twins of constancy, the Devil and Hearst!"

Smitten in spirit with a sudden shame,
And from intemperate exertion lame,
    I sprang, and skyward with a parting kick
Hoisted that mellow bulb, and left the game.

THE NEW ENOCH ARDEN

Enoch Arden was an able
    Seaman; hear of his mishap—
Not in wild mendacious fable,
    As 'twas told by t'other chap;

For I hold it is a youthful
    Indiscretion to tell lies,
And the writer that is truthful
    Has the reader that is wise.

Enoch Arden, able seaman,
    On an isle was cast away,
And before he was a free man
    Time had touched him up with gray.

Long he searched the far horizon,
    Seated on a mountain top;
Vessel ne'er he set his eyes on
    That would undertake to stop.

Seeing that his sight was growing
    Dim and dimmer day by day,

Enoch said he must be going.
  So he rose and went away—

Went away and so continued
  Till he lost his lonely isle:
Mr. Arden was so sinewed
  He could row for many a mile.

Compass he had not, nor sextant,
  To direct him o'er the sea:
Ere 'twas known that he was extant,
  At his boyhood's home was he.

When he saw the hills and hollows
  And the streets he could but know,
He gave utterance as follows
  To the sentiments below:

" Blast my tarry toplights! (shiver,
  Too, my timbers) but, I say,
W'at a larruk to diskiver
  That I've lost my blessed way!

" W'at, alas, would be my bloomin'
  Fate if Philip now I see,

Which I lammed?—or my old 'oman,
　Which has frequent basted *me?*"

All the landscape swam around him
　At the thought of such a lot:
In a swoon his Annie found him
　And conveyed him to her cot.

'Twas the very house, the garden,
　Where their honeymoon was passed:
'Twas the place where Mrs. Arden
　Would have mourned him to the last.

Ah, what grief she'd known without him!
　Now what tears of joy she shed!
Enoch Arden looked about him:
　" Shanghaied ! "—that was all he said.

DISAVOWAL

Two bodies are lying in Phœnix Park,
Grim and bloody and stiff and stark,
And a Land League man with averted eye
Crosses himself as he hurries by.
And he says to his conscience under his breath:
" I have had no hand in this deed of death."

A Fenian, making a circuit wide
And passing them by on the other side,
Shudders and crosses himself and cries:
"Who says that I did it, he lies, he lies!"
Gingerly stepping across the gore,
Pat Satan comes after the two before,
Makes, in a solemnly comical way,
The sign of the cross and is heard to say:
"O dear, what a terrible sight to see,
For babes like them and a saint like me!"
    1882.

AN AVERAGE

I ne'er could be entirely fond
Of any maiden who's a blonde,
And no brunette that e'er I saw
My whole devotion e'er could draw.

Yet sure no girl was ever made
Just half of light and half of shade.
And so, this happy mean to get,
I love a blonde and a brunette.

INCURABLE

From pride, guile, hate, greed, melancholy—
From any kind of vice, or folly,
Bias, propensity or passion
That is in prevalence and fashion,
Save one, the sufferer or lover
May, by the grace of God, recover.
Alone that spiritual tetter,
The zeal to make creation better,
Glows still immedicably warmer.
Who knows of a reformed reformer?

THE PUN

Hail, peerless Pun! thou last and best,
Most rare and excellent bequest
Of dying idiot to the wit
He died of, rat-like, in a pit!

Thyself disguised, in many a way,
Thou let'st thy sudden splendor play,
Adorning all where'er it turns,
As the revealing bull's-eye burns
For the dim thief, and plays its trick
Upon the lock he means to pick.

Yet sometimes, too, thou dost appear
As boldly as a brigadier
Tricke'd out with marks and signs all o'er
Of rank, brigade, division, corps,
To show by every means he can
An officer is not a man;
Or naked, with a lordly swagger,
Proud as a cur without a wagger,
Who says: " See simple worth prevail—
All dog, sir—not a bit of tail! "
'Tis then men give thee loudest welcome,
As if thou wert a soul from Hell come.

O obvious Pun! thou hast the grace
Of skeleton clock without a case—
With its whole boweling displayed,
And all its organs on parade.

Dear Pun, thou'rt common ground of bliss,
Where *Punch* and I can meet and kiss;
Than thee my wit can stoop no lower—
No higher his does ever soar.

TO NANINE

Dear, if I never saw your face again;
  If all the music of your voice were mute
  As that of a forlorn and broken lute;
If only in my dreams I might attain
The benediction of your touch, how vain
  Were Faith to justify the old pursuit
  Of happiness, or Reason to confute
The pessimist philosophy of pain.
Yet Love not altogether is unwise,
  For still the wind would murmur in the corn,
    And still the sun would splendor all the mere;
    And I—I could not, dearest, choose but hear
Your voice upon the breeze and see your eyes
  Shine in the glory of the summer morn.

VICE VERSA

Down in the state of Maine, the story goes,
  A woman, to secure a lapsing pension,
Married a soldier—though the good Lord knows
  That very common act scarce takes attention.

What makes it worthy to be writ and read—
The man she married had been nine hours dead!

Now, marrying a corpse is not an act
   Familiar to our daily observation,
And so I crave her pardon if the fact
   Suggests this interesting speculation:
Should some mischance restore the man to life
Would she be then a widow, or a wife?

Let casuists contest the point; I'm not
   Disposed to grapple with so great a matter.
'Twould tie my thinker in a double knot
   And drive me staring mad as any hatter—
Though I submit that hatters are, in fact,
Sane, and all other human beings cracked.

Small thought have I of Destiny or Chance;
   Luck seems to me the same thing as Intention;
In metaphysics I could ne'er advance,
   And think it of the Devil's own invention.
Enough of joy to know: Though when I wed
I *must* be married, yet I *may* be dead.

A BLACKLIST

" Resolved that we will post," the tradesmen say,
" All names of debtors who do never pay."
" Whose shall be first? " inquires the ready scribe—
" Who are the chiefs of the marauding tribe? "
Lo! high Parnassus, lifting from the plain,
Upon his hoary peak, a noble fane!
Within that temple all the names are scrolled
Of village bards, upon a slab of gold;
To that bad eminence, my friend, aspire,
And copy thou the Roll of Fame, entire.
Yet not to total shame those names devote,
But add in mercy this explaining note:
" These cheat because the law makes theft a crime,
And they obey all laws but laws of rhyme."

AUTHORITY

" Authority, authority! " they shout
Whose minds, not large enough to hold a doubt,
Some chance opinion ever entertain,
By dogma billeted upon their brain.
" Ha! " they exclaim with choreatic glee,
" Here's Dabster if you won't give in to me—

Dabster, sir, Dabster, to whom all men look
With reverence!" The fellow wrote a book.
It matters not that many another wight
Has thought more deeply, could more wisely write
On t'other side—that you yourself possess
Knowledge where Dabster did not badly guess.
God help you if ambitious to persuade
The fools who take opinions ready-made
And " recognize authorities." Be sure
No tittle of their folly they'll abjure
For all that you can say. But write it down,
Publish and die and get a great renown—
Faith! how they'll snap it up, misread, misquote,
Swear that they had a hand in all you wrote,
And ride your fame like monkeys on a goat!

THE PSORIAD

The King of Scotland, years and years ago,
Convened his courtiers in a gallant row
And thus addressed them:

"Gentle sirs, from you
Abundant counsel I have had, and true:
What laws to make to serve the public weal;
What laws of Nature's making to repeal;

What old religion is the only true one,
And what the greater merit of some new one;
What friends of yours my favor have forgot;
Which of your enemies against me plot.
In harvests ample to augment my treasures,
Behold the fruits of your sagacious measures!
The punctual planets, to their periods just,
Attest your wisdom and approve my trust.
Lo! the reward your faith and wisdom bring:
The grateful placemen bless their useful king!
But while you quaff the nectar of my favor
I mean somewhat to modify its flavor
By just infusing a peculiar dash
Of tonic bitter in the calabash.
And should you, too abstemious, disdain it,
Egad! I'll hold your noses till you drain it!

"You know, you dogs, your master long has felt
A keen distemper in the royal pelt—
A testy, superficial irritation,
Brought home, I fancy, from some foreign nation.
For this a thousand simples you've prescribed—
Unguents external, draughts to be imbibed.
You've plundered Scotland of its plants, the seas
You've ravished, and despoiled the Hebrides
To brew me remedies which, in probation,
Were sovereign only in their application.

In vain, and eke in pain, have I applied
Your flattering unctions to my soul and hide:
Physic and hope have been my daily food—
I've swallowed treacle by the holy rood!

"Your wisdom which sufficed to guide the year
And tame the seasons in their mad career,
When set to higher purposes has failed me
And added anguish to the ills that ailed me.
Nor that alone, but each ambitious leech
His rivals' skill has labored to impeach
By hints equivocal in secret speech.
For years, to conquer our respective broils,
We've plied each other with pacific oils
In vain: your turbulence is unallayed,
My flame unquenched; your quarreling unstayed;
My life so wretched from your strife to save it
That death were welcome did I dare to brave it.
With zeal inspired by your intemperate pranks,
My subjects muster in contending ranks.
Those fling their banners to the startled breeze
To champion some royal ointment; these
The standard of a royal purge display
And 'neath that ensign wage a wasteful fray!
Brave tongues are thundering from sea to sea,
Torrents of sweat roll reeking o'er the lea!
My people perish in their martial fear,
And rival bagpipes cleave the royal ear!

"Now, caitiffs, tremble, for this very hour
Your injured sovereign shall assert his power!
Behold this lotion, carefully compound
Of all the poisons you for me have found—
Of biting washes such as tan the skin,
And drastic drinks to vex the parts within.
What aggravates an ailment will produce—
I mean to rub you with this dreadful juice!
Divided counsels you no more shall hatch—
At last you shall unanimously scratch.
Kneel, villains, kneel, and doff your shirts—God
    bless us!
They'll seem, when you resume them, robes of Nessus!"

The sovereign ceased, and, sealing what he spoke,
From Arthur's Seat * confirming thunders broke.
The conscious culprits, to their fate resigned,
Sank to their knees, all piously inclined.
This act, from high Ben Lomond where she floats,
The thrifty goddess, Caledonia, notes.
Glibly as nimble sixpence, down she tilts
Headlong, and ravishes away their kilts,
Tears off each plaid and all their shirts discloses,
Removes each shirt and their broad backs exposes.
The king advanced—then cursing fled amain,
Dashing the phial to the stony plain

    * A famous height overlooking Edinburgh.

(Where't straight became a fountain brimming o'er,
Whence Father Tweed derives his liquid store)
For lo! already on each back sans stitch
The red sign manual of the Rosy Witch!

PEACE

When lion and lamb have together lain down
    Spectators cry out, all in chorus:
"The lamb doesn't shrink nor the lion frown—
    A miracle's working before us!"

But 'tis patent why Hot-head his wrath holds in,
    And Faint-heart her terror and loathing;
For the one's but an ass in a lion's skin,
    The other a wolf in sheep's clothing.

THANKSGIVING

The Superintendent of an Almshouse. A Pauper.

SUPERINTENDENT:
So *you're* unthankful—you'll not eat the bird?
You sit about the place all day and gird.

I understand you'll not attend the ball
That's to be given to-night in Pauper Hall.

PAUPER:

Why, that is true, precisely as you've heard:
I have no teeth and I will eat no bird.

SUPERINTENDENT:

Ah! see how good is Providence. Because
Of teeth He has denuded both your jaws
The fowl's made tender; you can overcome it
By suction; or at least—well, you can gum it,
Confirming thus the dictum of the preachers
That Providence is good to all His creatures—
Turkeys excepted. Come, ungrateful friend,
If our Thanksgiving dinner you'll attend
You shall say grace—ask God to bless at least
The soft and liquid portions of the feast.

PAUPER:

Without those teeth my speech is rather thick—
He'll hardly understand Gum Arabic.
No, I'll not dine to-day. As to the ball,
'Tis known to you that I've no legs at all.
I had the gout—hereditary; so,
As it could not be cornered in my toe
They cut my legs off in the fond belief
That shortening me would make my anguish brief.

Lacking my legs I could not prosecute
With any good advantage a pursuit;
And so, because my father chose to court
Heaven's favor with his ortolans and port
(Thanksgiving every day!) the Lord supplied
Saws for my legs, an almshouse for my pride
And, once a year, a bird for my inside.
No, I'll not dance—my light fantastic toe
Took to its heels some twenty years ago.
Some small repairs would be required for putting
My body on a saltatory footing.

[*Sings:*]

O the legless man's an unhappy chap—
    Tum-hi, tum-hi, tum-he o'haddy.
The favors o' fortune fall not in his lap—
    Tum-hi, tum-heedle-do hum.
The plums of office avoid his plate
No matter how much he may stump the State—
    Tum-hi, ho-heeee.
The grass grows never beneath his feet,
But he cannot hope to make both ends meet—
    Tum-hi.
With a gleeless eye and a somber heart,
He plays the rôle of his mortal part:
Wholly himself he can never be.
O, a soleless corporation is he!
    Tum.

SUPERINTENDENT:

The chapel bell is calling, thankless friend,
Balls you may not, but church you *shall,* attend.
Some recognition cannot be denied
To the great mercy that has turned aside
The sword of death from us and let it fall
Upon the people's necks in Montreal;
That spared our city, steeple, roof and dome,
And drowned the Texans out of house and home;
Blessed all our continent with peace, to flood
The Balkan with a cataclysm of blood.
Compared with blessings of so high degree,
Your private woes look mighty small—to me.

L'AUDACE

Daughter of God! Audacity divine—
Of clowns the terror and of brains the sign—
Not thou the inspirer of the rushing fool,
Not thine of idiots the vocal drool:
Thy bastard sister of the brow of brass,
Presumption, actuates the charging ass.
Sky-born Audacity! of thee who sings
Should strike with freer hand than mine the strings;
The notes should mount on pinions true and strong,
For thou, the subject, shouldst sustain the song,

Till angels lean from Heaven, a breathless throng!
Alas! with reeling heads and wavering tails,
They (notes, not angels) drop and the hymn fails;
The minstrel's tender fingers and his thumbs
Are torn to rags upon the lyre he strums.
Have done! the lofty thesis makes demand
For stronger voices and a harder hand—
Night-howling apes to make the notes aspire,
And Poet Riley's fist to slug the rebel wire!

THE GOD'S VIEW-POINT

Cheeta Raibama Chunder Sen,
The wisest and the best of men,
Betook him to the place where sat
With folded feet upon a mat
Of precious stones beneath a palm,
In sweet and everlasting calm,
That ancient and immortal gent,
The God of Rational Content.
As tranquil and unmoved as Fate,
The deity reposed in state,
With palm to palm and sole to sole,
And beaded breast and beetling jowl,
And belly spread upon his thighs,
And costly diamonds for eyes.

As Chunder Sen approached and knelt
To show the reverence he felt;
Then beat his head upon the sod
To prove his fealty to the god;
And then by gestures signified
The other sentiments inside;
The god's right eye (as Chunder Sen,
The wisest and the best of men,
Half-fancied) grew by just a thought
More narrow than it truly ought.
Yet still that prince of devotees,
Persistent upon bended knees
And elbows bored into the earth,
Declared the god's exceeding worth
And begged his favor. Then at last,
Within that cavernous and vast
Thoracic space was heard a sound
Like that of water underground—
A gurgling note that found a vent
At mouth of that Immortal Gent
In such a chuckle as no ear
Had e'er been privileged to hear!

Cheeta Raibama Chunder Sen,
The wisest, greatest, best of men,
Heard with a natural surprise
That mighty midriff improvise.

And greater yet the marvel was
When from between those massive jaws
Fell words to make the views more plain
The god was pleased to entertain:
"Cheeta Raibama Chunder Sen,"
So ran the rede in speech of men—
"Foremost of mortals in assent
To creed of Rational Content,
Why come you here to impetrate
A blessing on your scurvy pate?
Can you not rationally be
Content without disturbing me?
Can you not take a hint—a wink—
Of what of all this rot I think?
Is laughter lost upon you quite,
To check you in your pious rite?
What! know you not we gods protest
That all religion is a jest?
You take me seriously?—you
About me make a great ado
(When I but wish to be alone)
With attitudes supine and prone,
With genuflexions and with prayers,
And putting on of solemn airs,
To draw my mind from the survey
Of Rational Content away!
Learn once for all, if learn you can,

This truth, significant to man:
A pious person is by odds
The one most hateful to the gods."

Then stretching forth his great right hand,
Which shadowed all that sunny land,
The deity bestowed a touch
Which Chunder Sen not overmuch
Enjoyed—a touch divine that made
The sufferer hear stars! They played
And sang as on Creation's morn
When spheric harmony was born.

Cheeta Raibama Chunder Sen,
The most astonished man of men,
Fell straight asleep and when he woke
The deity nor moved nor spoke,
But sat beneath that ancient palm
In sweet and everlasting calm.

THE ÆSTHETES

The lily cranks, the lily cranks,
  The loppy, loony lasses!
They multiply in rising ranks
To execute their solemn pranks,
  They moon along in masses.
Blow, sweet lily, in the shade! O,
Sunflower decorate the dado!

The maiden ass, the maiden ass,
  The tall and tailless jenny!
In limp attire as green as grass,
She stands, a monumental brass,
  The one of one too many.
Blow, sweet lily, in the shade! O,
Sunflower decorate the dado!
  1883.

WITH MINE OWN PETARD

Time was the local poets sang their songs
Beneath their breath in terror of the thongs
I snapped about their shins. Though mild the stroke
Bards, like the conies, are " a feeble folk,"
Fearing all noises but the one they make
Themselves—at which all other mortals quake.
Now from their cracked and disobedient throats,
Like rats from sewers scampering, their notes
Pour forth to move, whene'er the season serves,
If not our legs to dance, at least our nerves;
As once a ram's-horn solo maddened all
The sober-minded stones of Jerich's wall.
A year's exemption from the critic's curse
Mends the bard's courage but impairs his verse.
Thus poolside frogs, when croaking in the night,
Are frayed to silence by a meteor's flight,
Or by the sudden plashing of a stone
From some adjacent cottage garden thrown,
But straight renew the song with double din
Whene'er the light goes out or man goes in.
Shall I with arms unbraced (my casque unlatched,
My falchion pawned, my buckler, too, attached)
Resume the cuishes and the broad cuirass,
Accomplishing my body all in brass,

And arm in battle-royal to oppose
A village poet singing through the nose?
No, let them rhyme; I fought them once before
And stilled their songs—but, Satan! how they swore!—
Cuffed them upon the mouth whene'er their throats
They cleared for action with their sweetest notes;
Twisted their ears (they'd oft tormented mine)
And damned them roundly all along the line;
Clubbed the whole crew from the Parnassian slopes,
A wreck of broken heads and broken hopes!
What gained I so?   I feathered every curse
Launched at the village bards with lilting verse.
The town approved and christened me (to show its
High admiration) Chief of Local Poets!

RESTORED

Dull were the days and sober,
  The mountains were brown and bare,
For the season was sad October
  And a dirge was in the air.

The mated starlings flew over
  To the isles of the southern sea.
She wept for her warrior lover—
  Wept and exclaimed: "Ah me!

" Long years have I mourned my darling
    In his battle-bed at rest;
And it's O, to be a starling,
    With a mate to share my nest!"

The angels pitied her sorrow,
    Restoring her warrior's life;
And he came to her arms on the morrow
    To claim her and take her to wife.

An aged lover—a portly,
    Bald lover, a trifle too stiff,
With manners that would have been courtly,
    And would have been graceful, if—

If the angels had only restored him
    Without the additional years
That had passed since the enemy bored him
    To death with their long, sharp spears.

As it was, he bored her, and she rambled
    Away with her father's young groom,
And the old lover smiled as he ambled
    Contentedly back to the tomb.

SIRES AND SONS

Wild wanton Luxury lays waste the land
With difficulty tilled by Thrift's hard hand!
Then dies the State!—and, in its carcass found,
The millionaires all maggot-like abound.
Alas! was it for this that Warren died,
And Arnold sold himself to t'other side,
Stark piled at Bennington his British dead,
And Gates at Camden, Lee at Monmouth, fled?—
For this that Perry did the foeman fleece,
And Hull surrender to preserve the peace?
Degenerate countrymen, renounce, I pray,
The slothful ease, the luxury, the gay
And gallant trappings of this idle life,
And be more fit for one another's wife.

A CHALLENGE

A bull imprisoned in a stall
Broke boldly the confining wall,
And found himself, when out of bounds,
Within a washerwoman's grounds.

There, hanging on a line to dry,
A crimson skirt inflamed his eye.
With bellowings that woke the dead,
He bent his formidable head,
With pointed horns and knurly forehead;
Then, planting firm his shoulders horrid,
Began, with rage made half insane,
To paw the arid earth amain,
Flinging the dust upon his flanks
In desolating clouds and banks,
The while his eyes' uneasy white
Betrayed his doubt what foe the bright
Red tent concealed, perchance, from sight.
The garment, which, all undismayed,
Had never paled a single shade,
Now found a tongue—a dangling sock,
Left carelessly inside the smock:
" I must insist, my gracious liege,
That you'll be pleased to raise the siege:
My colors I will never strike.
I know your sex—you're all alike.
Some small experience I've had—
You're not the first I've driven mad."

TWO SHOWS

The showman (blessing in a thousand shapes!)
Parades a " School of Educated Apes! "
Small education's needed, I opine,
Or native wit, to make a monkey shine.
The brute exhibited has naught to do
But ape the larger apes that come to view—
The hoodlum with his horrible grimace,
Long upper lip and furtive, shuffling pace,
Significant reminders of the time
When hunters, not policemen, made him climb;
The lady loafer with her draggling " trail,"
That free translation of an ancient tail;
The sand-lot quadrumane in hairy suit,
Whose heels are thumbs perverted by the boot;
The painted actress throwing down the gage
To elder artists of the sylvan stage,
Proving that in the time of Noah's flood
Two ape-skins held her whole profession's blood;
The critic waiting, like a hungry pup,
To write the school—perhaps to eat it—up,
As chance or luck occasion may reveal
To earn a dollar or maraud a meal.
To view the school of apes these creatures go,
Unconscious that themselves are half the show.

These, if the simian his course but trim
To copy them as they have copied him,
Will call him " educated." Of a verity
There's much to learn by studying posterity.

A POET'S HOPE

'Twas a weary-looking mortal, and he wandered near
    the portal
Of the melancholy City of the Discontented Dead.
He was pale and worn exceeding and his manner was
    unheeding,
    As if it could not matter what he did nor what he
    said.

" Sacred stranger,"—I addressed him with a reverence
    befitting
    The austere, unintermitting, dread solemnity he wore;
'Tis the custom, too, prevailing in the vicinage when
    hailing
    One who possibly may be a person lately " gone be-
    fore "—

" Sacred stranger, much I ponder on your evident de-
    jection,
    But my carefulest reflection leaves the riddle still
    unread.

How do you yourself explain your dismal tendency to
    wander
  By the melancholy City of the Discontented Dead?"

Then that solemn person, pausing in the march that
    he was making,
  Roused himself as if awaking, fixed his dull and
    stony eye
On my countenance and slowly, like a priest devout
    and holy,
  Chanted in a mournful monotone the following reply:

"O my brother, do not fear it; I'm no disembodied
    spirit—
  I am Lampton, the Slang Poet, with a price upon
    my head.
I am watching by this portal for some late lamented
    mortal
To arise in his disquietude and leave his earthy bed.

"Then I hope to take possession and pull in the earth
    above me
  And, renouncing my profession, ne'er be heard of any
    more.

For there's not a soul to love me and no living thing
respects me,
Which so painfully affects me that I fain would ' go
before.' "

Then I felt a deep compassion for the gentleman's de-
jection,
For privation of affection would refrigerate a frog.
So I said: "If nothing human—if neither man nor
woman
Can appreciate the fashion of your merit buy a dog."

THE WOMAN AND THE DEVIL

When Man and Woman had been made,
  All but the disposition,
The Devil to the workshop strayed,
  And somehow gained admission.

The Master rested from his work,
  For this was on a Sunday,
The man was snoring like a Turk,
  Content to wait till Monday.

"Too bad!" the Woman cried; "O, why,
  Does slumber not benumb me?
A disposition! Oh, I die
  To know if 'twill become me!"

The Adversary said: "No doubt
  'Twill be extremely fine, ma'am,
Though sure 'tis long to be without—
  I beg to lend you mine, ma'am."

The Devil's disposition when
  She'd got, of course she wore it,
For she'd no disposition then,
  Nor now has, to restore it.

TWO ROGUES

Dim, grim, and silent as a ghost,
The sentry occupied his post,
To all the stirrings of the night
Alert of ear and sharp of sight.
A sudden something—sight or sound,
About, above, or underground,
He knew not where nor what—ensued,
Thrilling the sleeping solitude.

The soldier cried: " Halt! Who goes there? "
The answer came: " Death—in the air."
" Advance, Death—give the countersign,
Or perish if you cross that line!"
To change his tone Death thought it wise—
Reminded him they'd been allies
Against the Russ, the Frank, the Turk,
In many a bloody bit of work.
" In short," said he, " in every weather
We've soldiered, you and I, together."
The sentry would not let him pass.
" Go back," he growled, "you tiresome ass—
Go back and rest till the next war,
Nor kill by methods all abhor:
Miasma, famine, filth and vice,
With plagues of locusts, plagues of lice,
Foul food, foul water, and foul gases,
Rank exhalations from morasses.
If you employ such low allies
This business you will vulgarize.
Renouncing then the field of fame
To wallow in a waste of shame,
I'll prostitute my strength and lurk
About the country doing work—
These hands to labor I'll devote,
Nor cut, by Heaven, another throat!"

THE PIED PIPER OF BROOKLYN

So, Beecher's dead. He was a great soul, too—
　Great as a giant organ is, whose reeds
　Hold in them all the souls of all the creeds
That man has ever taught and never knew.

When on this mighty instrument was laid
　His hand Who fashioned it, our common moan
　Was suppliant in its thundering. The tone
Grew more vivacious when the Devil played.

No more those luring harmonies we hear,
　And lo! already men forget the sound.
　They turn, retracing all the dubious ground
O'er which he'd led them stoutly by the ear.

NOT GUILTY

"I saw your charms in another's arms,"
　Said a Grecian swain with his blood a-boil;
"And he kissed you fair as he held you there,
　A willing bird in a serpent's coil!"

The maid looked up from the cinctured cup
　Wherein she was crushing the berries red,
Pain and surprise in her honest eyes—
　"It was only one o' those gods," she said.

PRESENTIMENT

With saintly grace and reverent tread,
  She walked among the graves with me;
  Her every foot-fall seemed to be
A benediction on the dead.

The guardian spirit of the place
  She seemed, and I some ghost forlorn
  Surprised in the untimely morn
She made with her resplendent face.

Moved by some waywardness of will,
  Three paces from the path apart
  She stepped and stood—my prescient heart
Was stricken with a passing chill.

The folk-lore of the years agone
  Remembering, I smiled and thought:
  " Who shudders suddenly at naught,
His grave is being trod upon."

But now I know that it was more
  Than idle fancy. O, my sweet,
  I did not think so little feet
Could make a buried heart so sore!

A STUDY IN GRAY

I step from the door with a shiver
  (This fog is uncommonly cold)
And ask myself: What did I give her?—
  The maiden a trifle gone-old,
  With the head of gray hair that was gold.

Ah, well, I suppose 'twas a dollar,
  And doubtless the change is correct,
Though it's odd that it seems so much smaller
  Than what I'd a right to expect.
  But you pay when you dine, I reflect.

So I walk up the street—'twas a saunter
  A score of years back, when I strolled
From this door; and our talk was all banter
  Those days when her hair was of gold,
  And the sea-fog less searching and cold.

A score? Why, that isn't so very
  Much time to have lost from a life.
There's reason enough to be merry:
  I've not fallen down in the strife,
  But marched with the drum and the fife.

If Hope, when she lured me and beckoned,
  Had pushed at my shoulders instead,
And Fame, on whose favors I reckoned,
  Had laureled the worthiest head,
  I could hallow the years that are dead.

Believe me, I've held my own, mostly
  Through all of this wild masquerade;
But somehow the fog is more ghostly
  To-night, and the skies are more grayed,
  Like the locks of the restaurant maid.

If ever I'd fainted and faltered
  I'd fancy this did but appear;
But the climate, I'm certain, has altered—
  Grown colder and more austere
  Than it was in that earlier year.

The lights, too, are strangely unsteady
  That lead from the street to the quay.
I think they'll go out—and I'm ready
  To follow. Out there in the sea
  The fog-bell is calling to me.

FOR MERIT

To Parmentier Parisians raise
　　A statue fine and large:
He cooked potatoes fifty ways,
　　Nor ever led a charge.

" *Palmam qui meruit*"—the rest
　　You know as well as I;
And best of all to him that best
　　Of sayings will apply.

Let meaner men the poet's bays
　　Or warrior's medal wear;
Who cooks potatoes fifty ways
　　Shall bear the palm—de terre.

A BIT OF SCIENCE

What! photograph in colors?   'Tis a dream
　　And he who dreams it is not overwise,
If colors are vibration they but seem,
　　And have no being.   But if Tyndall lies,
　　Why, come, then—photograph my lady's eyes.
Nay, friend, you can't; the splendor of their blue,

As on my own beclouded orbs they rest,
To naught but vibratory motion's due,
    As heart, head, limbs and all I am attest.
How could her eyes, at rest themselves, be making
In me so uncontrollable a shaking?
    1894.

THE TABLES TURNED

Over the man the street car ran,
    And the driver did never grin.
" O killer of men, pray tell me when
    Your laughter means to begin.

" Ten years to a day I've observed you slay,
    And I never have missed before
Your jubilant peals as your crunching wheels
    Were spattered with human gore.

" Why is it, my boy, that you smother your joy,
    And why do you make no sign
Of the merry mind that is dancing behind
    A solemner face than mine? "

The driver replied: " I would laugh till I cried
　　If I had bisected you;
But I'd like to explain, if I can for the pain,
　　'Tis myself that I've cut in two."

TO A DEJECTED POET

Thy gift, if that it be of God,
　　Thou hast no warrant to appraise,
　　Nor say: " Here part, O Muse, our ways,
The road too stony to be trod."

Not thine to call the labor hard
　　And the reward inadequate.
　　Who haggles o'er his hire with Fate
Is better bargainer than bard.

What! count the effort labor lost
　　When thy good angel holds the reed?
　　It were a sorry thing indeed
To stay him till thy palm be crossed.

" The laborer is worthy "—nay,
　　The sacred ministry of song
　　Is rapture!—'twere a grievous wrong
To fix a wages-rate for play.

THE HUMORIST

"What is that, mother?"
                    "The humorist, child.
His hands are black, but his heart is mild."

"May I touch him, mother?"
                    "'Twere needlessly done:
He is slightly touched already, my son."

"O, why does he wear such a ghastly grin?"
"'Tis the outward sign of a joke within."

"Will he crack it, mother?"
                    "Not so, my saint;
'Tis meant for the *Saturday Livercomplaint*."

"Does he suffer, mother?"
                    "God help him, yes!—
A thousand and fifty kinds of distress."

"What makes him sweat so?"
                    "The demons that lurk
In the fear of having to go to work."
"Why doesn't he end, then, his life with a rope?"
"Abolition of Hell has deprived him of hope."

MONTEFIORE

I saw—'twas in a dream the other night—
A man whose hair with age was thin and white:
   One hundred years had bettered by his birth,
And still his step was firm, his eye was bright.

Before him and about him pressed a crowd.
Each head in reverence was bared and bowed,
   And Jews and Gentiles in a hundred tongues
Extolled his deeds and spoke his fame aloud.

I joined the throng and, pushing forward, cried,
"Montefiore!" with the rest, and vied
   In efforts to caress the hand that ne'er
To want and worth had charity denied.

So closely round him swarmed our shouting clan
He scarce could breathe, and taking from a pan
   A gleaming coin, he tossed it o'er our heads,
And in a moment was a lonely man!

DISCRETION

SHE:

I'm told that men have sometimes got
  Too confidential, and
Have said to one another what
  They—well, you understand.
I hope I don't offend you, sweet,
But are you sure that you're discreet?

HE:

'Tis true, sometimes my friends in wine
  Their conquests do recall,
But none can truly say that mine
  Are known to him at all.
I never, never talk you o'er—
In truth, I never get the floor.

AN EXILE

'Tis the census enumerator
  A-singing all forlorn:
" It's ho! for the tall potater,
  And ho! for the clustered corn.

The whiffle-tree bends in the breeze and the fine
Large eggs are a-ripening on the vine.

" Some there must be to till the soil
   And the widow's weeds keep down.
I wasn't cut out for rural toil
   But they *won't* let me live in town!
They're not so many by two or three,
As they think, but ah! they're too many for me."

Thus the census man, bowed down with care,
   Warbled his wood-note high.
There was blood on his brow and blood in his hair,
   But he had no blood in his eye.

THE DIVISION SUPERINTENDENT

Baffled he stands upon the track—
The automatic switches clack.

Where'er he turns his solemn eyes
The interlocking signals rise.

The trains, before his visage pale,
Glide smoothly by, nor leave the rail.

No splinter-spitted victim he
Hears uttering the note high C.

In sorrow deep he hangs his head,
A-weary—would that he were dead.

Now suddenly his spirits rise—
A great thought kindles in his eyes.

Hope like a headlight's vivid glare,
Splendors the path of his despair.

His genius shines, the clouds roll back—
" I'll place obstructions on the track! "

TO A PROFESSIONAL EULOGIST

Newman, in you two parasites combine:
As tapeworm and as graveworm too you shine.
When on the virtues of the quick you've dwelt,
The pride of residence was all you felt
(What vain vulgarian the wish ne'er knew
To paint his lodging a flamboyant hue?)
And when the praises of the dead you've sung,
'Twas appetite, not truth, inspired your tongue;

As ill-bred men when warming to their wine
Boast of its merit though it be but brine.
Not gratitude incites your song, nor should—
Even Charity would shun you if she could.
You share, 'tis true, the rich man's daily dole,
But what you get you take by way of toll.
Vain to resist you—vermifuge alone
Has power to push you from your robber throne.
When to escape you he's compelled to die,
Hey! presto!—in the twinkling of an eye
You vanish as a tapeworm, reappear
As graveworm and resume your curst career.
As host no more, to satisfy your need
He serves as dinner your unaltered greed.
O thrifty sycophant to wealth and fame,
Son of servility and priest of shame,
While naught your mad ambition can abate
To lick the spittle of the rich and great;
While still like smoke your eulogies arise
To soot your heroes and inflame our eyes;
While still with holy oil, like that which ran
Down Aaron's beard, you smear each famous man,
I cannot choose but think it very odd
It ne'er occurs to you to fawn on God.

ELECTION DAY

Despots effete upon tottering thrones
Unsteadily poised upon dead men's bones,
Walk up! walk up! the circus is free,
And this wonderful spectacle you shall see:
Millions of voters who mostly are fools,
Demagogues' dupes and candidates' tools—
Armies of uniformed mountebanks,
And braying disciples of brainless cranks.
Many a week they've bellowed like beeves,
Bitterly blackguarding, lying like thieves,
Libeling freely the quick and the dead
And painting the New Jerusalem red.
Tyrants monarchical—emperors, kings,
Princes and nobles and all such things—
Noblemen, gentlemen, step this way:
There's nothing, the Devil excepted, to pay,
And the freaks and curios here to be seen
Are very uncommonly grand and serene.

No more with vivacity they debate,
Nor cheerfully crack the dissenting pate;
No longer, the dull understanding to aid,
The stomach accepts the instructive blade,

Nor the stubborn heart learns what is what
From a revelation of rabbit-shot;
And vilification's flames—behold!
Burn with a bickering faint and cold.

Magnificent spectacle!—every tongue
Suddenly civil that yesterday rung
(Like the clapper beating a brazen bell)
Each fair reputation's eternal knell;
Hands no longer delivering blows,
And noses, for counting, arrayed in rows.

Walk up, gentlemen—nothing to pay—
The Devil goes back to Hell to-day.

THE MILITIAMAN

" O warrior with the burnished arms,
    With bullion cord and tassel,
Pray tell me of the lurid charms
Of service and its fierce alarms:
    The storming of the castle,
The charge across the smoking field,
    The rifles' busy rattle—
What thoughts inspire the men who wield

The blade—their gallant souls how steeled
And fortified in battle."

" Nay, man of peace, seek not to know
   War's baleful fascination—
The soldier's hunger for the foe,
His dread of safety, joy to go
   To court annihilation.
Though calling bugles blow not now,
   Nor drums begin to beat yet,
One fear unmans me, I'll allow,
And poisons all my pleasure: How
   If I should get my feet wet!"

A WELCOME

Because you call yourselves Knights Templars, and
There's neither Knight nor Temple in the land,—
   Because you thus by vain pretense degrade
To paltry purposes traditions grand,—

Because to cheat the ignorant you say
The thing that's not, elated still to sway
   The crass credulity of gaping fools
And women by fantastical display,—

Because no sacred fires did ever warm
Your hearts, high knightly service to perform—
  A woman's breast or coffer of a man
The only citadel you dare to storm,—

Because while railing still at lord and peer,
At pomp and fuss-and-feathers while you jeer,
  Each member of your order tries to graft
A peacock's tail upon his barren rear,—

Because that all these things are thus and so,
I bid you welcome to our city. Lo!
  You're free to come, and free to stay, and free,
As soon as it shall please you, sirs—to go.

A SERENADE

" Σάς ἀγαπῶ, σάς ἀγαπῶ,"
    He sang beneath her lattice.
" ' Sas agapo ' ? " she murmured—" O,
    I wonder, now what *that* is ! "

Was she less fair that she did bear
    So light a load of knowledge?
Are tender looks got out of books,
    Or kisses taught in college?

Of woman's lore give me no more
　　Than how to love.　In many
A tongue men brawl; she speaks them all
　　Who says " I love," in any.

THE WISE AND GOOD

" O father, I saw at the church as I passed
The populace gathered in numbers so vast
That they cculdn't get in; and their voices were low,
And they looked as if suffering terrible woe."

" 'Twas the funeral, child, of a gentleman dead
For whom the great heart of humanity bled."

" What made it bleed, father, for every day
Somebody, somewhere, passes away?
Do the newspaper men print a column or more
Of every person whose troubles are o'er? "

" O, no; they could never do that—and indeed,
Though printers might print it, no reader would read.
To the sepulcher all, soon or late, must be borne,
But 'tis only the Wise and Good that we mourn."

" That's right, father dear, but how can our eyes
Distinguish in dead men the Good and the Wise? "

" That's easy enough to the stupidest mind:
They're poor, and in dying leave nothing behind."

" Seest thou in mine eye, father, anything green?
And takest thy son for a gaping marine?
Go tell thy fine tale of the Wise and the Good
Who are poor, yet lamented, to babes in the wood."

And that horrible youth as I hastened away
Was building a wink that affronted the day.

THE LOST COLONEL

" 'Tis a woful yarn," said the sailorman bold
    Who had sailed the northern lakes—
" No wofuler one has ever been told,
    Exceptin' them called ' fakes.' "

" Go on, thou son of the wind and fog,
    For I burn to know the worst! "
But his silent lip in a glass of grog
    Was dreamily immersed.

Then he wiped it upon his sleeve and said:
  " It's never like that I drinks
But what of a gallant gent that's dead
  I truly mournful thinks.

" He was a soldier chap—leastways
  As ' Colonel ' he was knew;
An' he hailed from some'rs where they raise
  A grass that's heavenly blue.

" He sailed as a passenger aboard
  The schooner ' Henery Jo.'
O wild the waves and galeses roared,
  Like taggers in a show!

"But he sat at table that calm an' mild
  As if he never had let
His sperit know that the waves was wild
  An' everlastin' wet!—

" Jest set with a bottle before his nose,
  As was labeled ' Total Eclipse '
(The bottle was) an' he frequent rose
  A glass o' the same to his lips.

" An' he says to me (for the steward slick
  Of the ' Henery Jo ' was I):

'This sailor life's the very old Nick—
   On the lakes it's powerful dry!'

"I says: 'Aye, aye, sir, it beats the Dutch.
   I hopes you'll outlast the trip.'
But if I'd been him—an' I said as much—
   I'd 'a' took a faster ship.

"His laughture, loud an' long an' free,
   Rang out o'er the tempest's roar.
'You're an elegant reasoner,' says he,
   'But it's powerful dry ashore!'"

"O mariner man, why pause and don
   A look of so deep concern?
Have another glass—go on, go on,
   For to know the worst I burn."

"One day he was leanin' over the rail,
   When his footing some way slipped,
An' (this is the wofulest part o' my tale)
   He was accidental unshipped!

"The empty boats was overboard hove,
   As he swum in the 'Henery's' wake;
But 'fore we had 'bouted ship he had drove
   From sight on the ragin' lake!"

"And so the poor gentleman was drowned—
And now I'm apprised of the worst."
"What! him? 'Twas an hour afore he was found—
In the yawl—stone dead o' thirst!"

FOR TAT

O heavenly powers! will wonders never cease?—
Hair upon dogs and feathers upon geese!
The boys in mischief and the pigs in mire!
The drinking water wet! the coal on fire!
In meadows, rivulets surpassing fair,
Forever running, yet forever there!
A tail appended to the gray baboon!
A person coming out of a saloon!
Last, and of all most marvelous to see,
A female Yahoo flinging filth at me!
If 'twould but stick I'd bear upon my coat
May Little's proof that she is fit to vote.

A DILEMMA

Filled with a zeal to serve my fellow men,
　For years I criticised their prose and verses:
Pointed out all their blunders of the pen,
Their shallowness of thought and feeling; then
　Damned them up hill and down with hearty curses!

They said: " That's all that he can do—just sneer,
　And pull to pieces and be analytic.
Why doesn't he himself, eschewing fear,
Publish a book or two, and so appear
　As one who has the right to be a critic?

" Let him who knows it all forbear to tell
　How little others know, but *show* his learning."
And then they added: " Who has written well
May censure freely "—quoting Pope. I fell
　Into the trap and books began out-turning,—

Books by the score—fine prose and poems fair,
　And not a book of them but was a terror,
They were so great and perfect; though I swear
I tried right hard to work in, here and there,
　(My nature still forbade) a fault or error.

'Tis true, some wretches, whom I'd scratched, no doubt,
  Professed to find—but that's a trifling matter.
Now, when the flood of noble books was out
I raised o'er all that land a joyous shout
  Till I was thought as mad as any hatter!

(Why hatters all are mad, I cannot say.
  'Twere wrong in their affliction to revile 'em,
But truly, you'll confess 'tis very sad
We wear the ugly things they make. Begad,
  They'd be less mischievous in an asylum!)

Consistency, thou art a—well, you're *paste!*
  When next I felt my demon in possession,
And made the field of authorship a waste,
All said of me: " What execrable taste,
  To rail at others of his own profession! "

Good Lord! where do the critic's rights begin
  Who has of literature some clear-cut notion,
And hears a voice from Heaven say: " Pitch in "?
He finds himself—alas, poor son of sin—
  Between the devil and the deep blue ocean!

METEMPSYCHOSIS

Once with Christ he entered Salem,
Once in Moab bullied Balaam,
Once by Apuleius staged
He the pious much enraged,
And, again, his head, as beaver,
Topped the neck of Nick the Weaver.
Omar saw him (minus tether—
Free and wanton as the weather:
Knowing naught of bit nor spur)
Stamping over Bahram-Gur.
Now, as Altgeld, see him joy
As Governor of Illinois!

THE SAINT AND THE MONK

Saint Peter at the gate of Heaven displayed
The tools and terrors of his awful trade;
The key, the frown as pitiless as night,
That slays intending trespassers at sight,
And, at his side in easy reach, the curled
Interrogation points all ready to be hurled.

Straight up the shining cloudway (it so chanced
No others were about) a soul advanced—
A fat, orbicular and jolly soul
With laughter-lines upon each rosy jowl—
A monk so prepossessing that the saint
Admired him, breathless until weak and faint,
Forgot his frown and all his questions too,
Foregoing even the customary " Who? "—
Threw wide the gate and with a friendly grin
Said: " 'Tis a very humble home, but pray walk in."

The soul smiled pleasantly. "Excuse me, please—
Who's in there? " By insensible degrees
This impudence dispelled the saint's esteem,
As dawning consciousness dispels a dream.
The frown began to blacken on his brow,
His hand to reach for "Whence? " and " Why? "
     and " How? "
" O, no offense, I hope," the soul explained;
" I'm rather—well, particular. I've strained
A point in coming here at all; 'tis said
That Susan Anthony (I hear she's dead
At last) and all her followers are here.
As company, they'd be—confess it—rather queer."

The saint replied, his rising anger past:
" What can I do?—the law is hard-and-fast,

Albeit unwritten and on earth unknown—
An oral order issued from the Throne:
By but one sin has Woman e'er incurred
God's wrath. To accuse Them Loud of that would be
    absurd."

That friar sighed, but, calling up a smile,
Said, slowly turning on his heel the while:
" Farewell, my friend. Put up the chain and bar—
I'm going, so please you, where the pretty women are."
    1895.

IN HIGH LIFE

Sir Impycu Lacquit, from over the sea,
Has led to the altar Miss Bloatie Bondee.
The wedding took place at the Church of St. Blare;
The fashion, the rank, and the wealth were all there.
No person was absent of all that one meets:
Lord Mammon himself bowed them into their seats,
While good Sir John Satan attended the door,
And Sexton Beëlzebub managed the floor,
Respectfully keeping each dog on its rug—
Preserving the peace between poodle and pug.

Twelve bridesmaids escorted the bride up the aisle,
To blush in her blush and to smile in her smile;
Twelve groomsmen supported the eminent groom,
To scowl in his scowl and to gloom in his gloom.
The rites were performed by the hand and the lip
Of his Grace the Diocesan, Osculo Grip
Assisted by three able-bodied divines;
He prayed and they grunted, he read, they made signs.
Such fashion, such beauty, such gowning, such grace
Were ne'er before seen in that heavenly place!
That night, full of gin and patrician pride,
Sir Impycu blackened the eyes of his bride.

A WHIPPER-IN

Commissioner of Pensions Dudley has established a Sunday-school and declares he will remove any clerk in his department who does not regularly attend.—*N. Y. World.*

Dudley, great placeman, man of mark and note,
   Worthy of honor from a feeble pen
   Blunted in service of all true, good men,
You serve the Lord—in courses, *table d'hôte*:
Au naturel, as well as *à la Nick*—
" Eat and be thankful, though it make you sick."

O, truly pious caterer, forbear
   To push the Saviour and Him crucified
   (*Brochette* you'd call it) into their inside
Who're all unused to such ambrosial fare.
The stomach of the soul makes quick revulsion
Of aught that it has taken on compulsion.

I search the Scripture, but I do not find
   That e'er the Spirit beats with angry wings
   For entrance to the heart, but sits and sings
To charm away the scruples of the mind.
It says: " Receive me, please; I'll not compel "—
Though if you don't you will go straight to Hell!

Well, that's compulsion, you will say.   'Tis true:
   We cower timidly beneath the rod
   Lifted in menace by an angry God,
But won't endure it from an ape like you.
Detested simian with thumb prehensile,
Switch *me* and I would brain you with my pencil!

Face you the Throne, nor dare to turn your back
   On its transplendency to flog some wight
   Who gropes and stumbles in the infernal night
Your ugly shadow lays along his track.
O, Thou who from the Temple scourged the sin,
Behold what rascals try to scourge it in!

JUDGMENT

I drew aside the Future's veil
    And saw upon his bier
The poet Whitman.   Loud the wail
    And damp the falling tear.

" He's dead—he is no more! " one cried,
    With sobs of sorrow crammed;
" No more?   He's this much more," replied
    Another: " he is damned! "
        1885.

A BUBBLE

Mrs. Mehitable Marcia Moore
    Was a dame of superior mind,
With a gown which, modestly fitting before,
    Was greatly puffed up behind.

The bustle she wore was ingeniously planned
    With an inspiration bright:
It magnified seven diameters and
    Was remarkably nice and light.

It was made of rubber and edged with lace
  And riveted all with brass,
And the whole immense interior space
  Inflated with hydrogen gas.

The ladies all said when she hove in view
  Like the round and rising moon:
"She's a stuck up thing!" which was partly true,
  And men called her the Captive Balloon.

To Manhattan Beach for a bath one day
  She went and she said: "O dear!
If I leave off *this* what will people say?
  I shall look so uncommonly queer!"

So a costume she had accordingly made
  To take it all nicely in,
And when she appeared in that suit arrayed,
  She was greeted with many a grin.

Proudly and happily looking around,
  She waded out into the wet;
But the water was very, very profound,
  And her feet and her forehead met!

As her bubble drifted away from the shore,
  On the glassy billows borne,

All cried: "Why, where is Mehitable Moore?
I saw her go in, I'll be sworn!"

Then the bulb it swelled as the sun grew hot,
  Till it burst with a sullen roar,
And the sea like oil closed over the spot—
  Farewell, O Mehitable Moore!

FRANCINE

Did I believe the angels soon would call
  You, my beloved, to the other shore,
  And I should never see you any more,
I love you so I know that I should fall
Into dejection utterly, and all
  Love's pretty pageantry, wherein we bore
  Twin banners bravely in the tumult's fore,
Would seem as shadows idling on a wall.
So daintily I love you that my love
  Endures no rumor of the winter's breath,
    And only blossoms for it thinks the sky
Forever gracious, and the stars above
  Forever friendly. Even the fear of death
    Were frost wherein its roses all would die.

AN EXAMPLE

They were two deaf mutes. They loved and they
    Resolved to be groom and bride;
And they listened to nothing that any could say,
    Nor ever a word replied.

From wedlock when warned by the married men,
    Maintain an invincible mind:
Be deaf and dumb until wedded—and then
    Be deaf and dumb and blind.

REVENGE

A spitcat sate on a garden gate
    And a snapdog fared beneath;
Careless and free was his mien, and he
    Held a fiddle-string in his teeth.

She marked his march, she wrought an arch
    Of her back and blew up her tail;
And her eyes were green as ever were seen,
    And she uttered a woful wail.

The spitcat's plaint was as follows: " It ain't
That I am to music a foe;
For fiddle-strings bide in my own inside,
And I twang them soft and low.

" But that dog has trifled with art and rifled
A kitten of mine, ah me!
That catgut slim was marauded from him:
'Tis the string that men call E."

Then she sounded high, in the key of Y,
A note that cracked the tombs;
And the missiles through the firmament flew
From adjacent sleeping-rooms.

As her gruesome yell from the gate-post fell
She followed it down to earth;
And that snapdog wears a placard that bears
The inscription: " Blind from birth."

THE GENESIS OF EMBARRASSMENT

When Adam first saw Eve he said:
" O lovely creature, share my bed."
Before consenting, she her gaze
Fixed on the greensward to appraise,
As well as vision could avouch,
The value of the proffered couch.
And seeing that the grass was green
And soft and scrupulously clean;
Observing that the flow'rs were rare
Varieties, and some were fair,
The posts of precious woods, and each
Bore luscious fruit in easy reach,
And all things suited well her worth,
She raised her angel eyes from earth
To his and, blushing to confess,
Murmured: " I love you, Adam—yes."
Since then her daughters, it is said,
Look always down when asked to wed.

IN CONTUMACIAM

Och! Father McGlynn,
Ye appear to be in
Fer a bit of a bout wid the Pope;
An' there's devil a doubt
But he's knockin' ye out
While ye're hangin' onto the rope.

An' soon ye'll lave home
To thravel to Rome,
For its bound to Canossa ye are.
Persistin' to shtay
When ye're ordered away—
Bedad! that is goin' too far!

FROM THE MINUTES

When, with the force of a ram that discharges its
    ponderous body
Straight at the rear elevation of the luckless culler of
    simples,
The foot of Herculean Kilgore—statesman of surname
    suggestive

Or carnage unspeakable!—lit like a missile solid, prodigious

Upon the Congressional door with a monstrous and mighty momentum,

Causing the vain ineffective bar to political freedom

To fly from its hinges, effacing the nasal excrescence of Dingley,

That luckless one, decently veiling the ruin with ready bandanna,

Lamented the loss of his eminence, sadly with sobs as follows:

" Ah, why was I ever elected to the halls of legislation,

So soon to be shown the door with pitiless emphasis?
    Truly,

I've leaned on a broken Reed, and the same has gone back on me meanly.

Where now is my prominence, erstwhile in council conspicuous, patent?

Alas, I did never before understand what now I see clearly,

To wit, that Democracy tends to level all human distinctions!"

A WOMAN IN POLITICS

What, madam, run for School Director? You?
    And want my vote and influence? Well, well,
That beats me! Gad! what *are* we coming to?
    In all my life I never have heard tell
    Of such sublime presumption, and I smell
A nigger in the fence! Excuse me, madam;
We statesmen sometimes speak like the old Adam.

But now you mention it—well, well, who knows?
    We might, that's certain, give the sex a show.
I have a cousin—teacher. I suppose
    If I stand in and you're elected—no?
    You'll make no bargains? That's a pretty go!
But understand that school administration
Belongs to politics, not education.

We'll pass the teacher deal; but it were wise
    To understand each other at the start.
You know my business—books and school supplies;
    You'd hardly, if elected, have the heart
    Some small advantage to deny me—part
Of all my profits to be yours. What? "Stealing"?
Please don't express yourself with so much feeling.

You pain me, truly. Now one question more.
  Suppose a fair young man should ask a place
As teacher—would you (pardon) shut the door
  Of the Department in his handsome face
  Until—I know not how to put the case—
Would you extort a kiss to pay your favor?
Good Lord! you laugh? I thought the matter graver.

Well, well, we can't do business, I suspect:
  A woman has no head for politics.
My profitable offers you reject
  And will not promise anything to fix
  Things right that civic saints and angels mix.
Good morning. Stay—I'm chaffing you, conceitedly.
Madam, I mean to vote for you—repeatedly.

A BALLAD OF PIKEVILLE

Down in Southern Arizona where the Gila monster
    thrives,
And the " Mescalero," gifted with a hundred thousand
    lives,
Every hour renounces one of them by drinking liquid
    flame—
The assassinating wassail that has given him his name;

Where the enterprising dealer in Caucasian hair is seen
To hold his harvest festival upon the village-green,
While the late lamented tenderfoot upon the plain is
   spread
With a sanguinary circle on the summit of his head;
Where the cactuses (or cacti) lift their lances in the sun,
And incautious jackass-rabbits come to sorrow as they
   run,
Lived a colony of settlers—old Missouri was the State
Where they formerly resided at a prehistoric date.

Now, the spot that had beeen chosen for this colonizing
   scheme
Was as waterless, believe me, as an Arizona stream.
The soil was naught but ashes, by the breezes driven
   free,
And an acre and a quarter were required to sprout a pea.
So agriculture languished, for the land would not pro-
   duce,
And for lack of water, whisky was the beverage in use—
Costly whisky, hauled in wagons many a weary, weary
   day,
Mostly needed by the drivers to sustain them on their
   way.
Wicked whisky! King of Evils! Why, O why did
   God create
Such a curse and thrust it on us in our inoffensive state?

Once a parson came among them, and a holy man was
    he;
With his ailing stomach whisky wouldn't anywise agree;
So he knelt upon the *mesa* and he prayed with all his
    chin
That the Lord would send them water or incline their
    hearts to gin.

Scarcely was the prayer concluded ere an earthquake
    shook the land,
And with copious effusion springs burst out on every
    hand!
Merrily the waters gurgled, and the shock which gave
    them birth
Fitly was by some declared a temperance movement of
    the earth.

Astounded by the miracle, the people met that night
To celebrate it properly by some religious rite;
And 'tis truthfully recorded that before the moon had
    sunk
Every man and every woman were devotionally drunk.

A half a standard gallon (says history) per head
Of the best Kentucky prime was at that ceremony shed.
O the glory of that country! O the happy, happy folk
By the might of prayer delivered from Nature's iron
    yoke!
Lo! the plains to the horizon all are yellowing with rye,
And the corn upon the hill-top lifts its banners to the
    sky!

Gone the wagons, gone the drivers, and the road is
    grown to grass,
Over which the incalescent Bourbon did aforetime pass.
Pikeville (that's the name they've given, in their wild,
    romantic way,
To that irrigation district) now distills, statistics say,
Something like a hundred gallons, out of each recurrent
    crop,
To the head of population—and consumes it, every drop!

AN AUGURY

Upon my desk a single spray,
    With starry blossoms fraught.
I write in many an idle way,
    Thinking one serious thought.

"O flowers, a fine Greek name ye bear,
    And with a fine Greek grace."
(Be still, O heart that turns to share
    The sunshine of a face.)

"Have ye no messages—no brief,
    Still sign: ' Despair,' or ' Hope '? "
A sudden stir of stem and leaf—
    A breath of heliotrope!

LUSUS POLITICUS

Come in, old gentleman. How do you do?
  Delighted, I'm sure, that you've called.
I'm a sociable sort of a chap and you
Are a pleasant-appearing person, too,
  With a head agreeably bald.
That's right—sit down in the scuttle of coal
  And put up your feet in a chair.
  It is better to have them there;
And I've always said that a hat of lead,
  Such as I see you wear,
Is a better hat than a hat of glass.
And your boots of brass
  Are a natural kind of boots, I swear.
" May you wipe your nose on a paper of pins? "
        Why, certainly, man, why not?
  I rather expected you'd do so before,
  When I saw you poking it in at the door.
        It's dev'lish hot—
The weather, I mean. " You are twins? "
Why, that was evident at the start,
  From the way that you paint your head
  In stripes of purple and red,
        With dots of yellow.
        That proves you a fellow
With a love of legitimate art.

" You've bitten a snake and are feeling bad "?
That's very sad,
But Longfellow's words I beg to recall:
Your lot is the common lot of all.
" Horses are trees and the moon is a sneeze "?
That, I fancy, is just as you please.
Some think that way, and others hold
The contrary view;
I never quite knew,
For the matter o' that,
When everything has been said.
May I offer this mat
If you *will* stand on your head?
I suppose I look to be upside down
From your present point of view.
It's a giddy old world, from king to clown.
And a topsy-turvy, too.
But, worthy and now uninverted old man,
You're built, at least, on a normal plan
If ever a truth I spoke.
Smoke?
Your air and conversation
Are a liberal education,
And your clothes, including the metal hat
And the brazen boots—what's that?
" You never could stomach a Democrat
Since General Jackson ran?

You're another sort, but you predict
That your party'll get consummately licked? "
Good God! what a queer old man!

BEREAVEMENT

A Countess (so they tell the tale)
Who dwelt of old in Arno's vale,
Where ladies, even of high degree,
Know more of love than of A, B, C,
Came once with a prodigious bribe
Unto the learned village scribe,
That most discreet and honest man
Who wrote for all the lover clan,
Nor e'er a secret had betrayed
Save when inadequately paid.
" Write me," she sobbed—" I pray thee do—
A book about the Prince di Giu—
A book of poetry in praise
Of all his works and all his ways;
The godlike grace of his address,
His more than woman's tenderness,
His courage stern and lack of guile,
The loves that wantoned in his smile.
So great he was, so rich and kind,
I'll not within a fortnight find

His equal as a lover. O,
My God! I shall be drowned in woe!"
"What! Prince di Giu is dead?" exclaimed
The honest man for letters famed,
The while he pocketed her gold;
"Of what?—if I may be so bold."
Fresh storms of tears the lady shed:
"I stabbed him fifty times," she said.

A PICKBRAIN

What! imitate me, friend? Suppose that you
With agony and difficulty do
What I do easily—what then? You've got
A style I heartily wish *I* had not.
If I from lack of sense and you from choice
Grieve the judicious and the unwise rejoice,
No equal censure our deserts will suit—
We both are fools, but you're an ape to boot!

THE NAVAL CONSTRUCTOR

He looked upon the ships as they
    All idly lay at anchor,
Their sides with gorgeous workmen gay—
    The riveter and planker—

Republicans and Democrats,
  Statesmen and politicians.
He saw the swarm of prudent rats
  Swimming for land positions.

He marked each " belted cruiser " fine,
  Her poddy life-belts floating
In tether where the hungry brine
  Impinged upon her coating.

He noted with a proud regard,
  As any of his class would,
The poplar mast and poplar yard
  Above the hull of bass-wood.

He saw the Eastlake frigate tall,
  With quaintly carven gable,
Hip-roof and dormer-window—all
  With ivy formidable.

In short, he saw our country's hope
  In best of all conditions—
Equipped, to the last spar and rope,
  By working politicians.

He boarded then the noblest ship
  And from the harbor glided.
" Adieu, adieu ! " fell from his lip.
  Verdict: " He suicided."
    1881.

DETECTED

In Congress once great Mowther shone,
  Debating weighty matters;
Now into an asylum thrown,
  He vacuously chatters.

If in that legislative hall
  His wisdom still he'd vented,
It never had been known at all
  That Mowther was demented.

BIMETALISM

Ben Bulger was a silver man,
  Though not a mine had he:
He thought it were a noble plan
  To make the coinage free.

" There hain't for years been sech a time,"
  Said Ben to his bull pup,
" For biz—the country's broke and I'm
  The hardest kind of up.

" The paper says that that's because
  The silver coins is sca'ce,
And that the chaps which makes the laws
  Puts gold ones in their place.

" They says them nations always be
  Most prosperatin' where
The wolume of the currency
  Ain't so disgustin' rare."

His dog, which hadn't breakfasted,
  Dissented from his view,
And wished that he could swell, instead,
  The volume of cold stew.

" Nobody'd put me up," said Ben,
  " With patriot galoots
Which benefits their feller men
  By playin' warious roots;

" But havin' all the tools about,
  I'm goin' to commence
A-turnin' silver dollars out
  Wuth eighty-seven cents.

" The feller takin' 'em can't whine;
  (No more, likewise, can I):
They're better than the genooine,
  Which mostly satisfy.

" It's only makin' coinage free,
  And mebby might augment
The wolume of the currency
  A noomerous per cent."

I don't quite see his error nor
  Malevolence prepense,
But fifteen years they gave him for
  That technical offense.

TWO METHODS

To bucks and ewes by the Good Shepherd fed
The Priest delivers masses for the dead,
And even from estrays outside the fold
Death for the masses he would not withhold.
The Parson, loth alike to free or kill,
Forsakes the souls already on the grill,
And, God's prerogative of mercy shamming,
Spares living sinners for a harder damning.

FOUNDATIONS OF THE STATE

Observe, dear Lord, what lively pranks
Are played by sentimental cranks!

First this one mounts his hinder hoofs
And brays the chimneys off the roofs;
Then that one, with exalted voice,
Expounds the thesis of his choice,
Our understandings to bombard,
Till all the window panes are starred!
A third augments the vocal shock
Till steeples to their bases rock,
Confessing, as they humbly nod,
They hear and mark the will of God.
A fourth in oral thunder vents
His pinching penury of sense
Till dogs with sympathetic howls,
And lowing cows, and cackling fowls,
Hens, geese, and all domestic birds,
Attest the terror of his words.
Cranks thus their intellects deflate
Of theories about the State.
This one avers 'tis built on Truth,
And that on Temperance. This youth
Declares that Science bears the pile;
That graybeard, with a holy smile,
Says Faith is the supporting stone;
While women swear that Love alone
Could so unflinchingly endure
The heavy load. And some are sure
The solemn state of Christian Wedlock
Is the indubitable bedrock.

Physicians once about the bed
Of one whose life was nearly sped
Blew up a disputatious breeze
About the cause of his disease:
This, that and t'other thing they blamed.
"Tut, tut!" the dying man exclaimed,
"What made me ill I do not care;
You've not an ounce of it, I'll swear.
And if you had the skill to make it
I'd see you hanged before I'd take it!"

AN IMPOSTOR

Must you, Carnegie, evermore explain
Your worth, and all the reasons give again
Why black and red are similarly white
And you and God identically right?
Still must our ears without redress submit
To hear you play the solemn hypocrite
Walking in spirit some high moral level,
Raising at once his eye-balls and the devil?
Great King of Cant! if Nature had but made
Your mouth without a tongue I ne'er had prayed
To have an earless head. Since she did not,
Bear me, ye whirlwinds, to some favored spot—
Some mountain pinnacle that sleeps in air
So delicately, mercifully rare

That when the fellow climbs that giddy hill,
As, for my sins, I know at last he will,
To utter twaddle in that void inane
His soundless organ he will play in **vain.**

FRANCE

Unhappy State! with horrors still to strive:
Thy Hugo dead, thy Boulanger alive;
A Prince who'd govern where he dares not
    dwell,
And who for power would his birthright sell—
Who, eager o'er his enemies to reign,
Grabs at the scepter and conceals the chain;
While pugnant factions mutually strive
By cutting throats to keep the land alive.
Perverse in passion, as in pride perverse—
To all a mistress, to thyself a curse;
Sweetheart of Europe! every sun's embrace
Matures the charm and poison of thy grace.
Yet time to thee nor peace nor wisdom brings:
In blood of citizens and blood of kings
The stones of thy stability are set,
And the fair fabric trembles at a threat.

A GUEST

Death, are you well? I trust you have no cough
   That's painful or in any way annoying—
No kidney trouble that may carry you off,
   Nor heart disease to keep you from enjoying
Your meals—and ours. 'Twere very sad indeed
To have to quit the busy life you lead.

You've been quite active lately for so old
   A person, and not very strong-appearing.
I'm apprehensive, somehow, that my bold,
   Bad brother gave you trouble in the spearing.
And my two friends—I fear, sir, that you ran
Quite hard for them, especially the man.

I crave your pardon: 'twas no fault of mine;
   If you are overworked I'm sorry, very.
Come in, old man, and have a glass of wine.
   What shall it be—madeira, port or sherry?
What! just a mug of blood? That's funny grog
To ask a friend for, eh? Well, take it, hog!

A FALSE PROPHECY

Dom Pedro, Emperor of far Brazil
(Whence coffee comes, and the three-cornered
    nut)
They say that you're imperially ill,
  And threatened with paralysis. Tut-tut!
  Though Emperors are mortal, nothing but
A nimble thunderbolt could catch and kill
A man predestined to depart this life
By the assassin's bullet, bomb or knife.

Sir, once there was a President who freed
  Four million slaves; and once there was a Czar
Who freed ten times as many serfs. Sins breed
  The means of punishment, and tyrants are
  Hurled headlong out of the triumphal car
If faster than the law allows they speed.
Lincoln and Alexander struck a rut;
You freed slaves too. Paralysis!—tut-tut.
  1885.

A SONG OF THE MANY

God's people sorely were oppressed,
   I heard their lamentations long;—
   I hear their singing, clear and strong,
I see their banners in the West!

The captains shout the battle-cry,
   The legions muster in their might;
   They turn their faces to the light,
They lift their arms, they testify:

" We sank beneath the masters' thong,
   Our chafing chains were ne'er undone;—
   Now clash your lances in the sun
And bless your banners with a song!

" God bides His time with patient eyes
   While tyrants build upon the land;—
   He lifts His face, He lifts His hand,
And from the stones His temples rise.

" Now Freedom waves her joyous wing
   Beyond the foemen's shields of gold.
   March forward singing, for, behold,
The right shall rule while God is King! "

ONE MORNING

Because that I am weak, my love, and ill
  I cannot follow the impatient feet
  Of my desire, but sit and watch the beat
Of the unpitying pendulum fulfill
The hour appointed for the air to thrill
  And brighten at your coming.   O my sweet,
  The tale of moments is at last complete—
The tryst is broken on the gusty hill!
O lady, faithful-footed, loyal-eyed,
  The long leagues silence me; yet doubt me not:
Think rather that the clock and sun have lied
  And all too early you have sought the spot.
For lo! despair has darkened all the light,
And till I see your face it still is night.

THE KING OF BORES

Abundant bores afflict this world, and some
  Are bores of magnitude that come and—no,
  They're always coming, but they never go—
Like funeral pageants, as they drone and hum
Their lurid nonsense like a muffled drum,

Or bagpipe's dread, unnecessary flow.
But one superb tormentor I can show—
Prince Fiddlefaddle, Duc de Feefawfum.
He the johndonkey is who, when I pen
    Amorous verses in an idle mood
        To nobody, or of her, reads them through
And, smirking, says he knows the lady; then
    Calls me sly dog. I wish he understood
    This tender sonnet's application too.

HISTORY

What wrecked the Roman power? One says vice,
Another indolence, another dice.
Emascle says polygamy. " Not so,"
Says Impycu—" 'twas luxury and show."
The parson, lifting up a brow of brass,
Swears superstition gave the *coup de grâce*.
Great Allison, the statesman-chap affirms
'Twas lack of coin (croaks Medico: " 'Twas
    worms! ")—
And John P. Jones the swift suggestion collars,
Averring the no coins were silver dollars.
Thus, through the ages, each presuming quack
Turns the poor corpse upon its rotten back,

Holds a new " autopsy " and finds that death
Resulted partly from the want of breath,
But chiefly from some visitation sad
That points his argument to serve his fad.
They're all in error—never human mind
The cause of the disaster has divined.
What slew the Roman power? Well, provided
You'll keep the secret, I will tell you.   I did.

THE HERMIT

To a hunter from the city,
    Overtaken by the night,
Spake, in tones of tender pity
    For himself, an aged wight:

" I have found the world a fountain
    Of deceit and Life a sham.
I have taken to the mountain
    And a Holy Hermit am.

" Sternly bent on Contemplation,
    Far apart from human kind—
In the hill my habitation,
    In the Infinite my mind.

"Ten long years I've lived a dumb thing,
　　Growing bald and bent with dole,
Vainly seeking for a Something
　　To engage my gloomy soul.

"Gentle Pilgrim, while my roots you
　　Eat, and quaff my simple drink,
Please suggest whatever suits you
　　As a Theme for me to Think."

Then the hunter answered gravely:
　　"From distraction free, and strife,
You could ponder very bravely
　　On the Vanity of Life."

"O, thou wise and learned Teacher,
　　You have solved the Problem well—
You have saved a grateful creature
　　From the agonies of Hell!

"Take another root, another
　　Cup of water: eat and drink.
Now I have a Subject, brother,
　　Tell me what, and how, to think."

THE YEARLY LIE

A merry Christmas? Prudent, as I live!—
You wish me something that you need not give.

Merry or sad, what does it signify?
To you 'tis equal if I laugh, or die.

Your hollow greeting, like a parrot's jest,
Finds all its meaning in the ear addressed.

Why " merry " Christmas? Faith, I'd rather frown
Than grin and caper like a tickled clown.

When fools are merry the judicious weep;
The wise are happy only when asleep.

A present? Pray you give it to disarm
A man more powerful to do you harm.

'Twas not your motive? Well, I cannot let
You pay for favors that you'll never get.

Perish the ancient custom of the gift,
Founded in terror and maintained in thrift!

What men of honor need to aid their weal
They purchase, or, occasion serving, steal.

Go celebrate the day with turkeys, pies,
Sermons and psalms and, for the children, lies.

Let Santa Claus descend again the flue;
If Baby doubt it, swear that it is true.

" A lie well stuck to is as good as truth,"
And God's too old to legislate for youth.

Hail Christmas! On my knees and fowl I fall;
For greater grace and better gravy call.
Vive l'Humbug!—that's to say, God bless us all!

AN APOLOGUE

A traveler observed one day
A loaded fruit-tree by the way,
And reining in his horse exclaimed:
" The man is greatly to be blamed
Who, careless of good morals, leaves
Temptation in the way of thieves.
Now lest some villain pass this way
And by this fruit be led astray
To bag it, I will kindly pack
It snugly in my saddle-sack."
He did so; then that Salt o' the Earth
Rode on, rejoicing in his worth.

DIAGNOSIS

Cried Allen Forman: "Doctor, pray
    Compose my spirit's strife:
O what may be my chances, say,
    Of living all my life?

"For lately I have dreamed of high
    And hempen dissolution!
O doctor, doctor, how can I
    Amend my constitution?"

The learned leech replied: "You're young
    And beautiful and strong—
Permit me to inspect your tongue:
    H'm, ah, ahem!—'tis long."

FALLEN

O, hadst thou died when thou wert great,
    When at thy feet a nation knelt
    To sob the gratitude it felt
And thank the Saviour of the State,
Gods might have envied thee thy fate!

Then was the laurel round thy brow,
    And friend and foe spake praise of thee,
    While all our hearts sang victory.
Alas! thou art too base to bow
To hide the shame that brands it now.

DIES IRÆ

A recent republication of the late Gen. John A. Dix's disappointing translation of this famous medieval hymn, together with some researches into its history, which I happened to be making at the time, induces me to undertake a translation myself. It may seem presumption in me to attempt that which so many eminent scholars of so many generations have attempted before me; but failure of others encourages me to hope that success, being still unachieved, is still achievable. The fault of many translations, from Lord Macaulay's to that of Gen. Dix, has been, I venture to think, a too strict literalness, whereby the delicate irony and subtle humor of the immortal poem—though doubtless these admirable qualities were valued by the translators—have been sacrificed in the result. In none of the English versions that I have examined is more than a trace of the mocking spirit of insincerity pervading the whole prayer,—the cool effrontery of the suppliant in enumerating his demerits, his serenely illogical demands of salvation in spite, or rather because, of them, his meek submission to the punishment of others, and the many similarly pleasing characteristics of this amusing work being most imper-

DIES IRÆ

Dies iræ! dies illa!
Solvet sæclum in favilla
Teste David cum Sibylla.

Quantus tremor est futurus,
Quando Judex est venturus.
Cuncta stricte discussurus.

fectly conveyed. By permitting myself a reasonable freedom of rendering—in many cases boldly supplying that "missing link" between the sublime and the ridiculous which the author, writing for the acute monkish apprehension of the thirteenth century, did not deem it necessary to insert—I have hoped at least partly to liberate the lurking devil of humor from his letters, letting him caper, not, certainly, as he does in the Latin, but as he probably would have done had his creator written in English. In preserving the meter and trochaic rhymes of the original, I have acted from the same reverent regard for the music with which, in the liturgy of the Church, the verses have become inseparably wedded that inspired Gen. Dix; seeking rather to surmount the obstacles to success by honest effort, than to avoid them by adopting an easier versification which would have deprived my version of all utility in religious service

I must bespeak the reader's charitable consideration in respect of the first stanza, the insuperable difficulties of which seem to have been purposely contrived in order to warn off trespassers at the very boundary of the alluring domain. I have got over the inhibition—somehow—but David and the Sibyl must try to forgive me if they find themselves represented merely by the names of those conspicuous personal qualities to which they probably owed their powers of prophecy, as Samson's strength lay in his hair.

THE DAY OF WRATH

Day of Satan's painful duty!
Earth shall vanish, hot and sooty;
So says Virtue, so says Beauty.

Ah! what terror shall be shaping
When the Judge the truth's undraping—
Cats from every bag escaping!

Tuba mirum spargens sonum
Per sepulchra regionem,
Coget omnes ante thronum.

Mors stupebit, et Natura,
Quum resurget creatura
Judicanti responsura.

Liber scriptus proferetur,
In quo totum continetur,
Unde mundus judicetur.

Judex ergo quum sedebit,
Quicquid latet apparebit,
Nil inultum remanebit.

Quid sum miser tunc dicturus,
Quem patronem rogaturus,
Quum vix justus sit securus?

Rex tremendæ majestatis,
Qui salvandos salvas gratis;
Salva me, Fons pietatis.

Recordare, Jesu pie,
Quod sum causa tuæ viæ;
Ne me perdas illa die.

Quærens me sedisti lassus
Redemisti crucem passus,
Tantus labor non sit cassus.

Now the trumpet's invocation
Calls the dead to condemnation;
All receive an invitation.

Death and Nature now are quaking,
And the late lamented, waking,
In their breezy shrouds are shaking.

Lo! the Ledger's leaves are stirring,
And the Clerk, to them referring,
Makes it awkward for the erring.

When the Judge appears in session,
We shall all attend confession,
Loudly preaching non-suppression

How shall I then make romances
Mitigating circumstances?
Even the just must take their chances.

King whose majesty amazes,
Save thou him who sings thy praises;
Fountain, quench my private blazes.

Pray remember, sacred Saviour,
Mine the playful hand that gave your
Death-blow. Pardon such behavior.

Seeking me, fatigue assailed thee,
Calvary's outlook naught availed thee;
Now 'twere cruel if I failed thee.

Juste Judex ultionis,
Donum fac remissionis
Ante diem rationis.

Ingemisco tanquam reus,
Culpa rubet vultus meus;
Supplicanti parce, Deus.

Qui Mariam absolvisti,
Et latronem exaudisti,
Mihi quoque spem dedisti.

Preces meæ non sunt dignæ,
Sed tu bonus fac benigne
Ne perenni cremer igne.

Inter oves locum præsta.
Et ab hædis me sequestra,
Statuens in parte dextra.

Confutatis maledictis,
Flammis acribus addictis,
Voca me cum benedictis.

Oro supplex et acclinis,
Cor contritum quasi cinis;
Gere curam mei finis.

Lacrymosa dies illa
Qua resurget et favilla,
Judicandus homo reus,
Huic ergo parce, Deus!

Righteous judge and learnèd brother,
Pray thy prejudices smother
Ere we meet to try each other.

Sighs of guilt my conscience gushes,
And my face vermilion flushes;
Spare me for my pretty blushes.

Thief and harlot, when repenting,
Thou forgavest—complimenting
Me with sign of like relenting.

If too bold is my petition
I'll receive with due submission
My dismissal—from perdition.

When thy sheep thou hast selected
From the goats, may I, respected,
Stand amongst them undetected.

When offenders are indicted,
And with trial-flames ignited,
Elsewhere I'll attend if cited.

Ashen-hearted, prone and prayerful,
When of death I see the air full,
Lest I perish too be careful.

On that day of lamentation,
When, to enjoy the conflagration,
Men come forth, O be not cruel:
Spare me, Lord—make them thy fuel.

ONE MOOD'S EXPRESSION

See, Lord, fanatics all arrayed
      For revolution!
To foil their villainous crusade
Unsheathe again the sacred blade
      Of persecution.

What though through long disuse 'tis grown
      A trifle rusty?
'Gainst modern heresy, whose bone
Is rotten, and the flesh fly-blown,
      It still is trusty.

Of sterner stuff, thine ancient foes,
      Unapprehensive,
Sprang forth to meet thy biting blows;
Our zealots chiefly to the nose
      Assume the offensive.

Then wield the blade their necks to hack,
      Nor ever spare one.
Thy crowns of martyrdom unpack,
But see that every martyr lack
      The head to wear one.

SOMETHING IN THE PAPERS

What's in the paper? " O, it's dev'lish dull:
There's nothing happening at all—a lull
After the war-storm. Mr. Someone's wife
Killed by her lover with, I think, a knife.
A fire on Blank Street and some babies—one,
Two, three or four, I don't remember, done
To quite a delicate and lovely brown.
A husband shot by woman of the town—
The same old story. Shipwreck somewhere south,
The crew all saved—or lost. Uncommon drouth
Makes hundreds homeless up the River Mud—
Though, come to think, I guess it was a flood.
'Tis feared some bank will burst—or else it won't;
They always burst I fancy—or they don't;
Who cares a cent?—the banker pays his coin
And takes his chances. Bullet in the groin—
But that's another item. Suicide—
Fool lost his money (serve him right) and died.
Heigh-ho! there's noth— Jerusalem! what's this?
Tom Jones has failed! My God, what an abyss
Of ruin!—owes me seven hundred, clear!
Was ever such a damned disastrous year?

THE BINNACLE

The Church possesses the unerring compass whose needle points directly and persistently to the star of the eternal law of God.—*Religious Weekly.*

The Church's compass, if you please,
Has two or three (or more) degrees
    Of variation;
And many a soul has gone to grief
On this or that or t'other reef
Through faith unreckoning or brief
    Miscalculation.
Misguidance is of perils chief
    To navigation.

The obsequious thing makes, too, you'll mark,
Obeisance through a little arc
    Of declination;
For Satan, fearing witches, drew
From Death's pale horse, one day, a shoe,
And nailed it to his door to undo
    Their machination.
Since then the needle dips to woo
    His habitation.

ONE PRESIDENT

"What are those, father?"   "Statesmen, my child—
Lachrymose, unparliamentary, wild."
"What are they that way for, father?"   "Last fall,
'Our candidate's better,' they said, 'than all!'"

"What did they say he was, father?"   "A man
Built on a straight and superior plan—
Believing that none for an office would do
Unless he were honest and capable too."

"Poor gentlemen—*so* disappointed!"   "Yes, lad,
That is the feeling that's driving them mad;
They're weeping and wailing and gnashing because
They find that he's all that they said that he was."

THE BRIDE

"You know, my friends, with what a brave carouse
I made a second marriage in my house—
    Divorced old barren Reason from my bed
And took the Daughter of the Vine to spouse."

So sang the Lord of Poets.   In a gleam
Of light that made her like an angel seem,
    The Daughter of the Vine said: "I myself
Am Reason, and the Other was a Dream."

THE MAN BORN BLIND

A man born blind received his sight
  By a painful operation;
And these are things he saw in the light
  Of an infant observation.

He saw a merchant, good and wise
  And greatly, too, respected,
Who looked, to those imperfect eyes,
  Like a swindler undetected.

He saw a patriot address
  A noisy public meeting.
He said: " Why, that's a calf, I guess,
  That for the teat is bleating."

A doctor stood beside a bed
  And shook his summit sadly.
" O see that foul assassin! " said
  The man that saw so badly.

He saw a lawyer pleading for
  A thief whom they'd been jailing,
And said: " That's an accomplice or
  My sight again is failing."

Upon the Bench a Justice sat,
  With nothing to restrain him;
" 'Tis strange," said the observer, " that
  They ventured to unchain him."

With theologic works suppplied,
  There was a solemn preacher;
" A burglar with his kit," he cried,
  " To rob a fellow creature."

A bluff old farmer next he saw
  Sell produce in a village,
And said: " What, what! is there no law
  To punish men for pillage?"

A dame, tall, fair and stately, passed,
  Who many charms united;
He thanked his stars his lot was cast
  Where sepulchers were whited.

He saw a soldier stiff and stern,
  " Full of strange oaths " and toddy,
But was unable to discern
  A wound upon his body.

Ten square leagues of rolling ground
  To one great man belonging,

Looked like one little grassy mound
With worms beneath it thronging.

A palace's well carven stones,
Where Dives dwelt contented,
Seemed built throughout of human bones
With human blood cemented.

He watched the shining yellow thread
A silk-worm was a-spinning;
"That creature's coining gold," he said,
"To pay some girl for sinning."

His eyes were so untrained and dim
All politics, religions,
Arts, sciences, appeared to him
But modes of plucking pigeons.

And as he drew his final breath,
He thought he saw with sorrow
Some persons weeping for his death
Who'd be all smiles to-morrow.

A NIGHTMARE

I dreamed that I was dead. The years went by:
The world remembered gratefully that I
　　Had lived and written, although other names
Once hailed with homage, had in turn to die.

Out of my grave a giant beech upgrew.
Its roots transpierced my body, through and through,
　　My substance fed its growth. From many lands
Men came in troops that noble tree to view.

'Twas sacred to my memory and fame—
But Julian Hawthorne's wittol daughter came
　　And with untidy finger daubed upon
Its bark a reeking record of her name.

A WET SEASON

Horas non numero nisi serenas.

The rain is fierce, it flogs the earth,
　　And man's in danger.
O that my mother at my birth
　　Had borne a stranger!

The flooded ground is all around,
    The depth uncommon.
How blest I'd be if only she
    Had borne a salmon!

If still denied the solar glow
    'Twere bliss ecstatic
To be amphibious—but O,
    To be aquatic!
We're worms, men say, o' the dust, and they
    That faith are firm of.
O, then, be just: show me some dust
    To be a worm of.

The pines are chanting overhead
    A psalm uncheering.
It's O, to have been for ages dead
    And hard of hearing!
Restore, ye Pow'rs, the last bright hours
    The dial reckoned;
'Twas in the time of Egypt's prime—
    Rameses II.

THE   CONFEDERATE   FLAGS

Tut-tut! give back the flags—how can you care,
  You veterans and heroes?
Why should you at a kind intention swear
  Like twenty Neros?

Suppose the act was not so overwise—
  Suppose it was illegal;
Is't well on such a question to arise
  And pinch the Eagle?

Nay, let's economize his breath to scold
  And terrify the alien
Who tackles him, as Hercules of old
  The bird Stymphalian.

Among the rebels when we made a breach
  Was it to get their banners?
That was but incidental—'twas to teach
  Them better manners.

They know the lesson well enough to-day;
  Now, let us try to show them
That we're not only stronger far than they,
  (How we did mow them!)

But more magnanimous. My lads, 'tis plain
    'Twas an uncommon riot;
The warlike tribes of Europe fight for gain;
    We fought for quiet.

If we were victors, then we all must live
    With the same flag above us;
'Twas all in vain unless we now forgive
    And make them love us.

Let kings keep trophies to display above
    Their doors like any savage;
The freeman's trophy is the foeman's love,
    Despite war's ravage.

" Make treason odious? " My friends, you'll find
    You can't, in right and reason,
While "Washington" and "treason" are combined—
    " Hugo " and " treason."

All human governments must take the chance
    And hazard of sedition.
O wretch! to pledge your manhood in advance
    To blind submission.

It may be wrong, it may be right, to rise
    In warlike insurrection:
The loyalty that fools so dearly prize
    May mean subjection.

Be loyal to your country, yes—but how
    If tyrants hold dominion?
The South believed they did; can't you allow
    For that opinion?

He who will never rise though rulers plot,
    His liberties despising—
How is he manlier than the *sans-culottes*
    Who's always rising?

Give back the foolish flags whose bearers fell,
    Too valiant to forsake them.
Is it presumptuous, this counsel? Well,
    I helped to take them.
        1891.

HÆC FABULA DOCET

A rat who'd gorged a box of bane
And suffered an internal pain
Came from his hole to die (the label
Required it if the rat were able)
And found outside his habitat
A limpid stream. Of bane and rat
'Twas all unconscious; in the sun
It ran and prattled just for fun.

Keen to allay his inward throes,
The beast immersed his filthy nose
And drank—then, bloated by the stream,
And filled with superheated steam,
Exploded with a rascal smell,
Remarking, as his fragments fell
Astonished in the brook: " I'm thinking
This water's damned unwholesome drinking! "

AGAIN

Well, I've met her again—at the Mission.
   She'd told me to see her no more;
It was not a command—a petition;
   I'd granted it once before.

Yes, granted it, hoping she'd write me,
   Repenting her virtuous freak—
Subdued myself daily and nightly
   For the better part of a week.

And then ('twas my duty to spare her
   The shame of recalling me) I
Just sought her again to prepare her
   For an everlasting good-bye.

O that evening of bliss—shall I ever
    Cease living it over?—although
She said, when 'twas ended: "You're never
    To see me again. And now go."

As we parted with kisses 'twas human
    And natural for me to smile
As I thought, "She's in love, and a woman:
    She'll send for me after a while."

But she didn't; so—well, the old Mission
    Is fine, picturesque and gray;
'Tis an excellent place for contrition—
    And sometimes she passes that way.

That's how it occurred that I met her,
    And that's all there is to tell—
Except that I'd like to forget her
    Calm way of remarking: "I'm well."

It was hardly worth while, all this keying
    My soul to such tensions and stirs
To learn that her food was agreeing
    With that little stomach of hers.

HOMO PODUNKENSIS

As the poor ass that from his paddock strays
Might sound abroad his field-companions' praise,
Recounting volubly their well-bred leer,
Their port impressive and their wealth of ear,
Mistaking for the world's assent the clang
Of echoes mocking his accurst harangue;
So the dull clown, untraveled though at large,
Visits the city on the ocean's marge,
Expands his eyes and marvels to remark
Each coastwise schooner and each alien bark;
Prates of "all nations", wonders as he stares
That native merchants sell imported wares,
Nor comprehends how in his very view
A foreign vessel has a foreign crew;
Yet, faithful to the hamlet of his birth,
Swears it superior to aught on earth,
Sighs for the temples locally renowned,
The village school-house and the village pound,
And chalks upon the palaces of Rome
The peasant sentiments of " Home, Sweet Home! "

A SOCIAL CALL

Well, well, old Father Christmas, is it you,
    With your thick neck and thin pretense of virtue?
Less redness in the nose—nay, even some blue,
    Would not, I think, particularly hurt you.
When seen close to, not mounted in your car,
You look the drunkard and the pig you are.

No matter, sit you down, for I am not
    In a gray study, as you sometimes find me.
Merry? O, no, nor wish to be, God wot,
    But there's another year of pain behind me.
That's something to be thankful for: the more
There are behind, the fewer are before.

I know you, Father Christmas, for a scamp,
    But Heaven endowed me at my soul's creation
With an affinity to every tramp
    That walks the world and steals its admiration.
For admiration is, like linen left
Upon the line, got easiest by theft.

Good God! old man, just think of it! I've stood,
    With brains and honesty, some five-and-twenty
Long years as champion of all that's good,
    And taken on the mazzard thwacks a-plenty.

Yet now whose praises do the people bawl?
Those of the fellows whom I live to maul.

Why, this is odd!—the more I try to talk
    Of you, the more my tongue grows egotistic
To prattle of myself! I'll try to balk
    Its waywardness and be more altruistic.
So let us speak of others—how they sin,
And what a devil of a state they're in!

That's all I have to say. Good-bye, old man.
    Next year you possibly may find me scolding—
Or miss me altogether: Nature's plan
    Includes, as I suppose, a final folding
Of these poor empty hands. Then drop a tear
To think they'll never box another ear.

MY DAY OF LIFE

I know not how it is——it seems
    Fantastic and surprising
That after all these dreams and dreams,
Here in the sun's first level beams,
    The sun is still just rising!

When first he showed his sovereign face,
    And bade the night-folk scuttle

Back to their holes, I took my place
Here on the hill, and God His grace
 Sent slumber soft and subtle.

Among the poppies red and white,
 I've lain and drowsed, for all it
Appears a sluggardly delight.
I must have had a wakeful night,
 Though, faith, I don't recall it.

And, O I've dreamed so many things!
 One hardly can unravel
The tangled web of visionings
That slumber-of-the-morning brings:
 Play, study, work and travel;

The love of women (mostly those
 Were fairest that were newest);
Hard knocks from friends and other foes:
Compacts with men (my memory shows
 The deadest are the truest);

War—what a hero I became
 By merely dreaming battle!
Athwart the field of letters, Fame
Blared through the brass my weary name
 With an ominous death-rattle.

Such an eternity of thought
  Within a minute's fraction!
Such phantoms out of nothing wrought,
And fading suddenly to naught
  As I awake to action!

They scamper each into its hole,
  These dreams of my begetting.
They've had their moment; take, my soul,
Thy day of life. . . . Gods! this is droll—
  That thieving sun is setting!

SOME ANTE-MORTEM EPITAPHS

A KING OF CRAFT

Here lies Sam Chamberlain; his fatal smile
Survives its wielder for a little while
In nightmares of the prudent few who fled
The Judas kisses that it heralded—
Those all are dreamless who stood still to view
The smile that stayed them for the stab that slew.
Against his God his warfare now is o'er:
His bloodless heart (no colder than before)
No longer with a mute ambition swells
To run a half-a-hundred little Hells.
With ever a polite, perfidious art—
A dove in manner and a snake in heart,
This titmouse Machiavelli ne'er again
Will feel the urge, the passion and the strain
To prove it true that one may smile and smile
And be a Chamberlain the blessed while.

    Sharp at both ends, his secret soul
    Was like a double-headed mole
    Equipped with equal nose to prod
    This way or that beneath the sod.
    Conjecture fitted to confound
    If seen a moment out of ground—

Its former, as its future, route
The matter of a vain dispute,
Save where a dunghill's lure supplied
Its aid the riddle to decide.
When that occurred (his nearer nose
Pointing the way with happier throes)
He sought it as a bee the rose.
And as that robber daubs its thighs
With pollen till it cannot rise,
So he, with glutted mind, remained
Inert, and Christ arose and reigned.

We raise the stone, we carve the solemn word,
The sign of promise and the symbol grim;
His voice and vice are in the land unheard—
  Yet all is doubtful that relates to him.
No more he twirls his smile to work us woe;
  We saw him put a fathom under sod:
  Flung down at last—but so was Aaron's rod.
We *hope* he's dead, but only this we know:
  He does not smile. O glory be to God!

STEPHEN DORSEY

Flee, heedless stranger, from this spot accurst,
Where rests in Satan an offender first
In point of greatness, as in point of time,
Of new-school rascals who proclaim their crime.

Skilled with a frank loquacity to blab
The dark arcana of each mighty grab,
And famed for lying from his early youth,
He sinned secure behind a veil of truth.
Some lock their lips upon their deeds; some write
A damning record and conceal from sight;
Some, with a lust of speaking, die to quell it.
His way to keep a secret was to tell it.

MR. JUSTICE FIELD

Here sleeps one of the greatest students
                              Of jurisprudence.
Nature endowed him with the gift
                              Of juristhrift.
All points of law alike he threw
                              The dice to settle.
Those honest cubes were loaded true
                              With railway metal.

GENERAL B. F. BUTLER

Thy flesh to earth, thy soul to God,
   We gave, O gallant brother;
And o'er thy grave the awkward squad
   Fired into one another!

REPARATION

Beneath this monument which rears its head,
A giant note of admiration—dead,
His life extinguished like a taper's flame,
John Ericsson is lying in his fame.
Behold how massive is the lofty shaft;
How fine the product of the sculptor's craft;
The gold how lavishly applied; the great
Man's statue how impressive and sedate!
Think what the cost was! It would ill become
Our modesty to specify the sum;
Suffice it that a fair per cent. we're giving
Of what we robbed him of when he was living.

DISINCORPORATED

Of Corporal Tanner the head and the trunk
Are here in unconsecrate ground duly sunk.
His legs in the South claim the patriot's tear,
But, stranger, you needn't be blubbering here.

A KIT

Here Ingalls, sorrowing, has laid
The tools of his infernal trade—
His pen and tongue. So sharp they grew,
And such destruction from them flew,
His hand was wounded when he wrote,
And when he spoke he cut his throat.

DISJUNCTUS

Within this humble mausoleum
  Poor Guiteau's flesh you'll find.
His bones are kept in a museum,
  And Tillman has his mind.

A TRENCHER-KNIGHT

Stranger, uncover; here you have in view
The monument of Chauncey M. Depew,
Eater and orator, the whole world round
For feats of tongue and tooth alike renowned.
Dining his way to eminence, he rowed

With knife and fork up water-ways that flowed
From lakes of favor—pulled with all his force
And found each river sweeter than the source.

Like rats, obscure beneath a kitchen floor,
Gnawing and rising till obscure no more,
He ate his way to eminence, and Fame
Inscribes in gravy his immortal name.

A trencher-knight, he, mounted on his belly,
So spurred his charger that its sides were jelly.
Grown desperate at last, it reared and threw him,
And Indigestion, overtaking, slew him.

A VICE-PRESIDENT

Here the remains of Schuyler Colfax lie;
Born, all the world knows when, and God knows
    why.
In '71 he filled the public eye,
In '72 he bade the world good-bye;
In God's good time, with a protesting sigh,
He came to life just long enough to die.

A WASTED LIFE

Of Morgan here lies the unspirited clay,
Who secrets of Masonry swore to betray.
He joined the great Order and studied with zeal
The awful arcana he meant to reveal.
At last in chagrin by his own hand he fell—
There was nothing to learn, there was nothing to
    tell.
The Masons are said to have killed him. Not so—
Even a secret so foul, they're compelled to forego.

THE SCRAP HEAP

POESY

Successive bards pursue Ambition's fire
That shines, Oblivion, above thy mire.
The latest mounts his predecessor's trunk,
And sinks his brother ere himself is sunk.
So die ingloriously Fame's *élite,*
But dams of dunces keep the line complete.

HOSPITALITY

Why ask me, Gastrogogue, to dine,
(Unless to praise your rascal wine)
Yet never ask some luckless sinner
Who needs, as I do not, a dinner?

MAGNANIMITY

"To the will of the people we loyally bow!"
That's the minority shibboleth now.
O noble antagonists, answer me flat—
What would you do if you didn't do that?

357

UNDERSTATED

" I'm sorry I married," says Upton Sinclair:
" The conjugal status is awful!—
The devil's device, a delusion and snare."
Worse, far worse than that—it is lawful!

AN ATTORNEY-GENERAL

Philander Knox!—I know him by the sound;
His sleep, unlike his learning, is profound.
No dreams of duty mar his loud repose,
Nor strain the cobwebs tethering his nose,
Which, roaring ever like the solemn sea,
Proclaims to all the world that this is he.
In thought a tortoise but in act a hare,
Slow to decide and impotent to dare,
Yet no important crisis he ignores,
But sleeps upon it, and for action—snores.

FINANCIAL NEWS

Says Rockefeller: " Money is not tight,"
And, faith, I'm thinking that the man is right.
If it were not, at least in morals, loose
He hardly could command it for his use.

ASPIRATION

No man can truthfully say that he would not like to be
President.—*William C. Whitney.*

> Lo! the wild rabbit, happy in the pride
> Of qualities to meaner beasts denied,
> Surveys the ass with reverence and fear,
> Adoring his superior length of ear,
> And says: "No living creature, lean or fat,
> But wishes in his heart to be like That!"

DEMOCRACY

> Let slaves and subjects with extolling psalms
> Before their sovereign execute salaams;
> The freeman scorns one idol to adore—
> Tom, Dick, and Harry and himself are four.

AN ENEMY TO LAW AND ORDER

> A is defrauded of his land by B,
> Who's driven from the premises by C.
> D buys the place with coin of plundered E.
> "That A's an Anarchist!" says F to G.

FORESIGHT

An " actors' cemetery ! " Sure
The devil never tires
Of planning places to procure
The sticks to feed his fires.

A FAIR DIVISION

Another Irish landlord gone to grass,
Slain by the bullets of the tenant class!
Pray, good agrarians, what wrong requires
Such foul redress? Between you and the squires
All Ireland's parted with an even hand—
For you have all the ire, they all the land.

A LACKING FACTOR

" You acted unwisely," I cried, " as you see
By the outcome." He calmly eyed me:
" When choosing the course of my action," said he,
" I had not the outcome to guide me."

THE POLITICIAN

Let patriots manipulate
The tiller of the Ship of State;
Be mine the humble, useful toil
To work the tiller of the soil.

ELIHU ROOT

Stoop to a dirty trick or low misdeed?
    What, bend him from his moral skies to it?
No, no, not he!   To serve his nature's need
    He may upon occasion rise to it.

AN ERROR

" I never have been able to determine
Just how it is that the judicial ermine
Is safely guarded from predacious vermin."
" It is not so, my friend; though in a garret
'Tis kept in camphor, and you often air it,
The vermin will get into it and wear it."

VANISHED AT COCK-CROW

" I've found the secret of your charm," I said,
    Expounding with complacency my guess.
Alas! the charm, even as I named it, fled,
    For all its secret was unconsciousness.

WOMAN

Study good women and ignore the rest,
For he best knows the sex who knows the best.

A PARTISAN'S PROTEST

O statesmen, what would you be at,
    With torches, flags and bands?
You make me first throw up my hat,
    And then my hands.

A BEQUEST TO MUSIC

"Let music flourish!" So he said and died.
  Hark! when he's gone the minstrelsy begins:
The symphonies ascend, a swelling tide,
Melodious thunders fill the welkin wide—
  The grand old lawyers, chinning on their chins!

ONEIROMANCY

I fell asleep and dreamed that I
Was flung, like Vulcan, from the sky;
Like him, was lamed—another part:
His leg was crippled, and my heart.
I woke in time to see my love
Conceal a letter in her glove.

JULY FOURTH

God said: "Let there be noise." The dawning
  fire
Of Independence gilded every spire.

A PARADOX

" If life were not worth living," said the preacher,
" 'Twould have in suicide one pleasant feature."
"An error," said the pessimist, " you're making:
What's not worth having cannot be worth taking."

REEDIFIED

Lord of the Tempest, pray refrain
From leveling this church again.
Now in its doom, since so you've willed it,
We acquiesce; but *you'll* rebuild it.

A BULLETIN

" Lothario is very low,"
    So all the doctors tell.
Nay, nay, not so,—he will be, though,
    If ever he get well.

AN INSCRIPTION

For a Statue of Napoleon

A conqueror as provident as brave,
He robbed the cradle to supply the grave.
His reign laid quantities of human dust:
He fell upon the just and the unjust.

AN ERRONEOUS ASSUMPTION

Good for he's old?   Ah, Youth, you do not dream
How sweet the roses in the autumn seem!

A CONSTRUCTOR

I saw the devil.   He was working free—
A customs-house he builded by the sea.
"Why do you this?"   The devil raised his head:
"Of churches I have built enough," he said.

GOD COMPLIES

" By prayer see Megapomp restored,"
  Shouts Martext, pious creature.
Yes, God by supplication bored
  From every droning preacher,
Exclaimed: " So be it, tiresome crew;
But I've a crow to pick with you."

IN ARTICULO MORTIS

The paper presented he solemnly signed,
  Gasping—perhaps 'twas a jest he meant:
" This of a sound and disposing mind
  Is the last illwill and contestament."

THE DISCOVERERS

My! how my fame rings out in ever zone—
A thousand critics shouting: " He's unknown! "

UNEXPOUNDED

On Evidence, on Deeds, on Bills,
On Copyhold, on Loans, on Wills,
Lawyers great books indite.
The creaking of their busy quills
  I never heard on Right.

THE EASTERN QUESTION

Looking across the line, the Grecian said:
"This border I will stain a Turkey red."
The Moslem smiled serenely and replied:
"No Greek has ever for his country dyed."
While thus each patriot guarded his frontier
The Powers stole the country in his rear.

TWO TYPES

Courageous fool!—the peril's strength unknown.
Courageous man!—so conscious of your own.

TO A CRITIC OF TENNYSON

Affronting fool, subdue your transient light;
When Wisdom's dull dares Folly to be bright?
If Genius stumble in the path to fame
'Tis decency in dunces to go lame.

COOPERATION

No more the swindler singly seeks his prey:
To hunt in couples is the modern way—
A rascal from the public to purloin,
An honest man to hide away the coin.

HUMILITY

Great poets fire the world with fagots big
    That make a crackling racket,
But I'm content with but a whispering twig
    To warm some single jacket.

STRAINED RELATIONS

Says England to Germany: "Africa's ours."
    Says Germany: "Ours, I opine."
Says Africa: " Tell me, delectable Powers,
    What is it that ought to be mine?"

EXONERATION

When men at candidacy don't connive,
  From that suspicion if their friends would free 'em
The teeth and nails with which they do not strive
  Should be exhibited in a museum.

AFTER PORTSMOUTH

Begirt with bombs that fall and flames that rise,
The Tsar, bewildered, stares. "Alas," he cries,
"Life withholds joy and death denies release!
And Roosevelt would have me think this peace."

A VOICE FROM PEKIN

" ' Empress of China '! I nor rule nor reign:
I wear the purple but to hide the chain—
Free only to hold back the open door
For foreign devils drunk upon my floor."

A PIOUS RITE

On Maunday Thursday, as was good and meet,
The Emperor of Austria washed the feet
Of twelve poor men to show how humble he
For twenty minutes of the year could be.
O Thou, who trackest tenants of the throne
Through moral quagmires, make them wash their own.

JUSTICE

She jilted me. I madly cried:
   "The grave at least can hold her!"
Reflecting then that if she died
   'Twould stop her growing older,
I pitilessly sheathed the knife
And sternly sentenced her to life!

AT THE BEACH

List, England, to our words of scorn
For noblemen to title born!
Yet be thine eyes awhile depressed,
For one has turned his prow to-west,
And we, to catch his landing-line,
Are pickling all our shins in brine.

AN INFRACTION OF THE RULES

A duel in France, and the victor pursued
By the dogs of the law, by the multitude,
  By society's fierce ill-will!
O what is the matter? The man was so rude,
That he made an attempt to kill!

CONVERSELY

There's grief in Belgrade, for no crown, it is said,
  Is found for King Peter in all of the town.
How sad that he's lacking a crown for his head!
  How sweet were he lacking a head for his crown!

A WARNING

Cried Age to Youth: "Abate your speed!
The distance hither's brief indeed."
But Youth pressed on without delay—
The shout had reached but half the way.

PSYCHOGRAPHS

Says Gerald Massey: "When I write, a band
Of souls of the departed guides my hand."
How strange that poems cumbering our shelves,
Penned by immortal parts, have none themselves!

FOR WOUNDS

O bear me, gods, to some enchanted isle
Where woman's tears can antidote her smile.

A LITERARY METHOD

His "Hoosier poems" Riley says he writes
Upon an empty stomach. Heavenly Powers,
Feed him throat-full; for what the wretch indites
Upon his empty stomach empties ours!

BACK TO NATURE

Nathaniel, Julian, Hildegardy!
Sure the stock is far from hardy,
And the name once heard with awe
Now provokes the loud guffaw—
" Hawthorne " in the memory dear,
" Haw-haw-hawthorne " in the ear!

RUDOLPH BLOCK

What parallel, neighbor, be pleased to expound
'Twixt Belgium's king and you may be found?
Why this: if the cable dispatches are true
He lies on his deathbed. So would you.

BOYCOTT

" This thing's a bomb," said Gompers, lighting
The fuse; " 'twill blow them all a kiting! "
Well, now 'tis shattered all to pieces,
And Gompers but a spot of grease is.

TO HER

O Sinner A, to me unknown
Be such a conscience as your own!
To ease it, you to Sinner B
Confess the sins of Sinner C.

CREATION

God dreamed—the suns sprang flaming into place,
And sailing worlds with many a venturous race!
He woke—His smile alone illumined space.

REBUKE

When Admonition's hand essays
    Our greed to curse,
Its lifted finger oft displays
    Our missing purse.

PRAYER

Fear not in any tongue to call
Upon the Lord—He's skilled in all.
But if He answereth my plea
He speaketh one unknown to me.

THE LONG FEAR

Noting the hangman's frown and the law's righteous
    rage,
Our murderers live in terror till they die of age.

AN INSPIRED PERFORMANCE

The Devil troubled a pool of mud,
    And Vierick from out the smother
Arose and to prove his royal blood
    Defamed his peasant mother.
Dear Devil, his poems—we'll suffer all those,
But do not again provoke him to prose.

SEPULTURE

" Let's bury the hatchet," said Miller to Platt;
And Platt said to Miller: " I'll gladly do that."
On its grave, Warner Miller, the grasses grow not,
But the wind in your hair whistles over the spot.